Alex –
I have greatly enjoyed
getting to work with you.
Thank you for your friendship
and support and enjoy
your coaching journey!

Your Friend –

Chick

What Others are Saying:

"Chick and Mike have collaborated on writing the real deal. It is pragmatic, insightful and relevant. The subject of coaching is a challenge to properly define; Chick and Mike have broken the code. This book is a must for every manager. It will drive organizations to perform better."

Suku Radia – ***CEO and President, Bankers Trust***

"*It Begs the Question* provides invaluable insights that can be used by anyone in a management position to develop the full potential of their team. The beneficial impacts of Question-Centric Coaching will be clearly evident in a more positively motivated, productive organization; that will have higher morale, and greater levels of accomplishment. If you use the techniques provided in this book, on a daily basis, you will be a better leader."

Garry White – ***Rear Admiral, United States Navy (Retired)***

"As Chief Development Officer of one of America's leading media companies, I constantly am looking for tools to ensure that my team succeeds in a hyper-competitive market. I also place a high value on management techniques to provide to the many digital and new media businesses we acquire. *It Begs the Question* is a truly unique and powerful approach to better business leadership and more effective management, whatever the size of the organization."

John Zieser – ***Chief Development Officer and General Counsel, Meredith Corporation***

"A must read for any leader that believes all organizational success is achieved with and through people. Given today's economic uncertainty, the QCC process helps leaders ignite the passion of their people, gaining emotional and rational engagement that will drive higher levels of performance for the entire team! QCC is critical to inspiring a cross-generational, multi-cultural workforce to leverage their strengths and achieve peak performance."

Thomas J. Mahoney, Jr. – President & CEO, ITA Group

What Others are Saying:

"Initially Question-Centric Coaching felt counterintuitive to the concept of coaching, as I felt the role of the coach was to provide answers and direction to others. But experience with QCC has persuaded me it promotes accountability for the development of the agenda and actions by the person being coached. I find this critical to successful coaching relationships and outcomes."

Jeffrey B. Crandall, MD, FACP – ***Medical Director, Physician Development, UnityPoint Health System***

"I was hooked on this book from the initial chapter. For years these two high-powered business people made measurable improvements to organizations by leveraging a proven and repeatable process. When they discovered something they weren't expecting - the real impetus for this book was generated. The principles succinctly described here will have a significant impact on people and companies worldwide. "

Tim Herbert – ***Senior Partner Manager, ARM***

"This book should be a requirement of every manager who has the privilege of leading other people. The strategies and tactics provided are a "how to" for effective coaching. This is the first book I've encountered that provides tangible examples and strategies to maximize coaching time for managers. It's truly a "must read" if you want to lead a successful team."

Steve Jermier – ***Vice President Sales, Wells Fargo Retail Services***

It begs the question

Learn how the best managers drive performance through Question-Centric Coaching

Chick Herbert & Mike McCoy

For general inquiries, or to order additional books, please visit www.questioncentriccoaching.com

Cataloging-in-Publication Data is on file with the Library of Congress
ISBN: 978-0-9899856-0-4 (PB)
ISBN: 978-0-9899856-1-1 (EB)
Book design by Craig Tassin and Levelbdesign
Printed in the United States of America
First Edition: January 2014

This book is dedicated to our families for their love and support.

Acknowledgements

We have been blessed to spend time with a multitude of very successful people. Our approach when interacting with these individuals has always been to observe their leadership styles and understand the attributes that make them strong leaders. This book represents a compilation of lessons learned from the many men and women who influenced us over the course of our careers. No one becomes successful on their own and we are indebted to those who have invested in our personal and professional development.

Special thanks to Steve Keay for his countless contributions. Steve was instrumental in making this book a reality and we are so appreciative of him generously sharing his time and expertise. Steve's insight and intellect were invaluable at every step of our journey and we always walked away from our meetings with expanded knowledge and a renewed vigor for completing this project.

Thank you to the many business associates, friends, and family who read our manuscript and provided valuable feedback along the way. We are so appreciative for the thorough review provided early in the process by Mike Volkema, Rear Admiral Garry White (Ret.), Erik Fyrwald, Jerry Stone, Mary Vermeer Andringa, Julie White, John Zieser, Steve Jermier, Tim herbert and Dr. Jeffrey Crandall.

Special thanks to the outstanding editing of Susie Dunn Bentley; her input early on had a significant impact on the grammar, flow and content. As we worked toward the finish line we benefited from having two individuals who take their craft very seriously. The first person is Sheri Cooper, who performed a comprehensive proofreading of our final manuscript. Just when we thought things were coming together from a content perspective, Sheri's annotations quickly reminded us that our grammar was far from perfect! We were fortunate to work with a great creative mind in Craig Tassin from Level B Design (www.levelbdesign.com). Craig did a wonderful job of successfully bringing together the cover and interior book design in a manner that represented our original vision.

Additionally Chick would like to acknowledge:

I want to begin by thanking my family. My wife Shari is an amazing person and I am so thankful for her continued confidence, support and unwavering love. Her encouragement around the writing of this book kept me moving forward during those times when it would have been easy to hang things up and call it quits. My three sons, Trey, Kyle and Quinn, also played a key role in this effort. They inspired me with the genuine excitement they displayed about me writing a book. They consistently asked how the book was coming and when it would be done. The fear of letting them down was great motivation to me

I was raised by an incredible mother and father; Charles "Chick" and Adrienne Herbert. As I progress in my career, my admiration for my father continues to grow. The way he mentored young architects in his firm and granted them significant responsibility and opportunities for growth was decades ahead of its time. Concepts taught by the current list of leadership gurus reflect nearly an identical approach to what my dad was doing decades ago before it was in vogue. That includes the power of asking strategic questions. My dad leaves behind a wonderful legacy and one which makes me immensely proud to be his namesake.

My mother was an equally amazing person. She taught me many things and was always there to support me when I made good and bad decisions. Her devotion to giving back to the community had a significant impact on my desire to volunteer. She was admired by many and went about life with a faith based principled approach. She taught me about humility and perseverance as I watched her fight in a long battle with cancer. She was always more concerned how everyone else was doing over her own health and well-being. My mother continues to be an inspiration to me and I only wish she was still with us.

Thank you to Dr. Bob Gelina who generously passed along his wealth of knowledge in the areas of organizational development, understanding the psychological elements of human interaction and the concepts of continuous improvement and statistical process control. Bob dedicated significant time towards my professional development and made learning fun and exciting. Bob shaped the early part of my career and his teachings continue to influence my actions all these years later. I am so thankful he hired me as a young and inexperienced associate back in 1992.

Thank you to Tim Freeman with Efficient Marketing, Incorporated. I can't adequately articulate how much Tim shaped my career and taught me about the role of a true consultant. I walked away from each and every conversation with Tim better equipped to do my job and help others develop their critical thinking skills. He was a master coach, asked powerful questions and challenged my thinking. The three and a half years we worked together were some of the best years of my career. I only wish I had the same level of interactions with Tim today as I did from 2008 to 2011.

Thank you to my middle brother Tim Herbert. Tim has been an inspiration to me from a very early age. While always close, it wasn't until I joined the professional ranks that I began to understand and appreciate the many talents he possessed as a business person. The successes he has earned through hard work inspire me. He is my number one fan and is always the first person I call when I need professional insight about an important decision. He has been so generous to our family over the years and a huge influence on every aspect of my life, including the writing of this book.

Lastly, I want to thank my co-author, Mike McCoy. Mike has been a tremendous mentor and friend to me over the years. He has taught me many things and continues to be a significant influence in my life. I have great appreciation for his big ideas, marketing savvy, and his generous and giving personality. He has been, and will continue to be a great friend for many years to come.

Additionally Mike would like to acknowledge:

Let me begin by thanking my wife Rhonda and our three sons Mitch, Mason and Miller, for their support, assistance and cheerleading.

Rhonda's proofreading and grammar checks were very helpful. Her support and understanding for the weekend time I dedicated to this effort was even more important. She was an inspiration to me and her love and confidence gave me the focus to finish the project.

I want to thank my boys for their ongoing interest in writing the book. Their questions and support were very important to me and I sincerely appreciate it. I can't thank them enough for caring and being a big part of my motivation.

I've been extremely fortunate to work with some great leaders over my career. They coached me, taught me, showed me grace when I made a mistake and took a personal interest in me. These amazing people include but are not limited to Jerry Stone, Randy Bray, Dave Kvamme, Tom Shippee, and Suka Radia. These leaders demonstrated ethics in action, smart decision making and a genuine interest in the people they worked with; all important qualities for any leader to emulate.

An important thank you goes to my good friend and co-author Chick Herbert. Every time we became delayed by events in our careers and in our family life he found a way to get us jumpstarted! Not only did I enjoy our time together writing our book, I also looked forward to our conversations about our families, especially our sons which are near each other in age and school. I look forward to continuing these conversations for years into the future.

Table of Contents

Section 1:
The Fundamentals of Coaching

Section 2
The Fundamentals of Questions

Section 3

Implementing the Fundamentals

Section 4

The Turbo-Charged Results

Introduction

If you are like us, you probably don't have much time to read the latest management and leadership books. Your time is at a premium. As a result, personal time you can invest in self-improvement or professional development is limited. Yet, you are continuously expected to achieve greater results utilizing fewer resources. There has never been a more critical time for managers to operate from a different playbook, yet where does one turn to find a more effective model? How does an individual transform himself from good manager to great coach, and what are the benefits of doing so? You know that finding and implementing those few key concepts that actually work are worth their weight in gold. The question is how to find them. So, as succinctly as possible, let us share with you what this book is all about.

This book is about dramatically improving team and personal performance, exerting less effort than you're investing today, and ensuring the sustainability of the improvements you make. When your management team is asking the right questions at the right time in the right way, your managers and team members will achieve higher performance levels and, as a result, more personal success.

Our experience is that of practitioners, not consultants. We have witnessed firsthand the positive outcomes resulting from enhanced coaching. This book represents a compilation of knowledge and experience gained throughout many years in both large and small organizations. We have tested and implemented these approaches in various industries, across complex and geographically dispersed teams, in centralized and decentralized environments, and in both business-to-business and consumer-related businesses. Our goal in this book is to translate this experience with hundreds of managers into straightforward lessons you can put into practice immediately.

As a result of following the process and using the tools in this book, you will perform at a higher level, your organization will experience better results, and you will create additional time in your day to reinvest in those activities that make the most difference in performance. These strategies will function as your personal turbo-charger to generate extra power, or significant improvement over the norm. While these strategies are the right thing to do in good times, they are imperative in difficult times.

As you move through the chapters, you will learn in a few hours what took us years to discover and perfect. Through our work, we discovered four major cornerstones of Question-Centric Coaching.

1. Work "on" versus "in" the system – The best coaches know how to create an environment that makes their team successful rather than always "coming to the rescue" and doing the team's work for them.
2. Becoming a Level 3 Coach – The best coaches differentiate themselves by mastering the attributes and skills of Level 3 Coaches.
3. Use leverage to create change – Once great coaches harness the principles of leverage, they make positive change occur much faster for individuals, teams and organizations.
4. Develop others to be Level 3 Coaches – The best coaches know how to develop others into Level 3 Coaches to create long-term sustainability.

In the end, our goal is that you will emerge as a more productive coach with improved coaching skills and be better prepared to lead your organization to a level of performance far beyond where it is today.

SECTION I

The Fundamentals of Coaching

Chapter 1
The Power of Coaching

Prior to capturing our findings for this book, we spent years intimately involved with numerous organizations across the country. Our objective in these engagements was to sift through the processes used by companies in a wide range of industries and identify those activities, tools, and behaviors that, if focused on, would lead to improved results. Then we partnered with these companies to implement our findings and recommendations. Every time we did this, performance improved.

Our approach clearly worked. At this point in the journey it would have been easy to declare victory and go home. However, as we continued to observe and interact with our clients over time, we noticed that while performance was better with all of them, they divided themselves into two distinct groups. This was something we weren't expecting. After experiencing significant improvement in results, Group One reached a plateau while Group Two continued to improve. As we studied this phenomenon, we came to view this point of departure as the Turbo-Charger Effect.

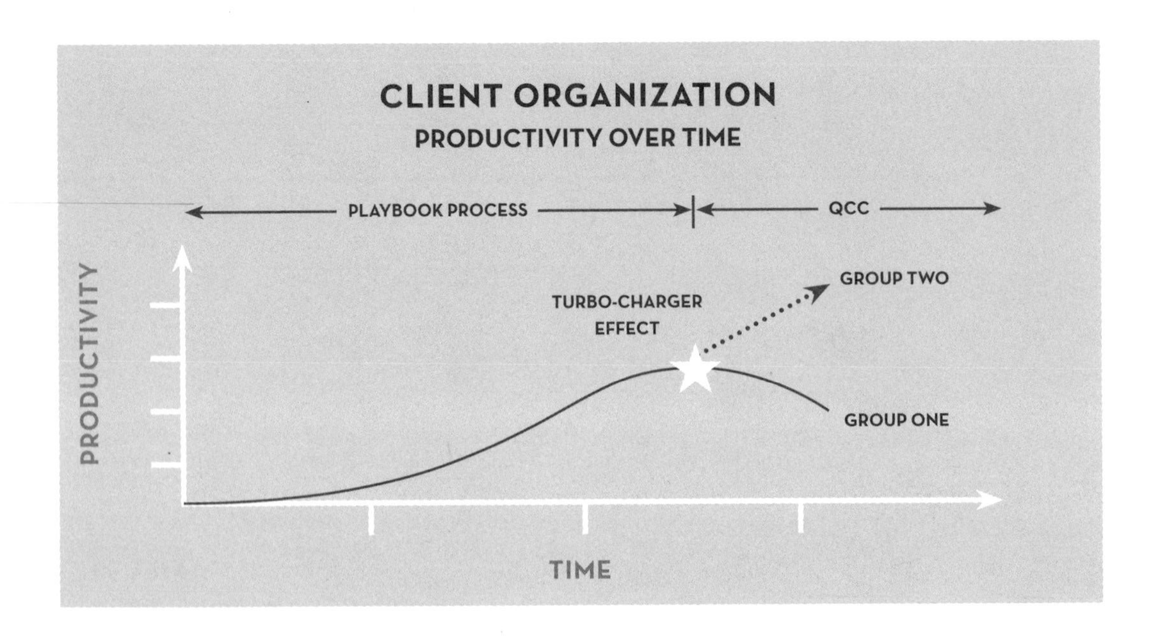

The previous diagram illustrates the Turbo-Charger Effect and the point of separation in terms of productivity between the two groups.

After further evaluation, here's what we found. Our initial work with new organizations was focused on interviews with employees, uncovering best practices and identifying critical activities that drove performance improvement. In partnership with our clients, we developed solutions that institutionalized the key processes and behaviors that lifted productivity of the entire team. We created a vocabulary, tools, measurement, and a way of viewing the business that drove success.

Our early focus was on three things:

1. Identify the key activities that improved business results
2. Document these activities in a Playbook
3. Focus on the flawless execution of plays in the Playbook

The Value of Coaching

While this formula drove success, it did not explain what happened at the point of departure where Group Two separated itself from Group One. We dug in and discovered that performance coaching was the distinguishing factor between the two groups. Managers, teams, and organizations that separated from the pack, excelled at coaching. Suffice it to say we are not talking about rah-rah, slap you on the back, go "win one for the Gipper" coaching. Relevant coaching improves performance beyond where one can go alone. Our specific coaching strategy instills critical thinking skills, is input driven, collaborative, and focused on the individual. Most importantly, it involves questions; lots of questions. Subsequently, we came to call this approach, Question-Centric Coaching or QCC. It was the difference maker.

In a brief moment, our forty-plus years of combined experience and intense focus on driving performance improvement crystallized. It became apparent that the critical success factor was both the amazing power of QCC and the broad applicability of the concept. Everything you are about to learn in this book is rooted in the concepts of QCC and the QCC system, which allows managers to achieve outstanding results by boosting both individual and team performance.

Learning Question-Centric Coaching

Great execution requires developing new skills and changing old habits and behaviors. Since change can be difficult, this book is organized into four easy-to-digest sections that make it simple to refer back to key concepts.

Section One introduces you to the **Fundamentals of Coaching**. Chapters in this section focus on the power and benefits of coaching, the differences between managing and coaching, and the importance of both. In addition, this section introduces the core elements of QCC, including the Coaching Conversation Process© and learning about the importance of predictability, relevancy, and reaching mutual agreement. Here you will be introduced to the powerful concept that distinguishes the best managers from the rest of the pack by the activities that receive their time and attention.

Section Two focuses on the **Fundamentals of Questions** and builds on the foundation laid in Section One. Here you will delve more deeply into the power and effectiveness of QCC. You will participate in role-plays that demonstrate the importance of building trust and learn ways in which you can build trust with those that you coach. You will learn about the Question Continuum© and then how to use questions in coaching sessions to diagnose problems, determine satisfaction levels of those being coached, and, most importantly, how to get people to willingly spring into action after coaching sessions.

The third section is dedicated to making you more effective, both individually and as a manager, by **Implementing the Fundamentals** learned in sections one and two. Your personal productivity gets turbo-charged as does your contribution to a project, team or organization. Chapters in this section release the secrets of working "on" the system versus "in" the system. Professionals who execute this strategy outperform those managers that toil "in" the system performing less valuable activities. You will be armed with tools to maximize your productivity. Additionally, you will be introduced to the powerful concept of leverage. You will learn how to create and maximize leverage to improve both your personal performance and the performance of your team.

Finally, the fourth and final section details the **turbo-charged results** you can expect to see as you implement QCC. Throughout, you will be challenged to identify areas where you can improve. As with any change, you need to understand and communicate the benefits before you attempt to alter your team's behaviors and before your team is willing to sign on to the effort. As you learn the skills to become a more effective coach, you will learn why change may be desirable even if you've experienced success in your career to date.

Chapter 2

The Four Cornerstones of QCC

Coaching is critical to improving individual performance, building a collaborative culture, and addressing small problems before they blow up into large ones. In other words, it is something we do for the benefit of others. But is coaching only the time we take out of our busy schedules to selflessly help others?

As you will discover, effective coaching can have a dramatic impact not only on your team but also on your own performance and well-being. In particular, by using the tools of QCC, you will be able to:

1. Work "on" the system rather than "in" the system
2. Become a Level 3 Coach and improve the performance of your team
3. Use leverage to achieve greater change
4. Develop others into Level 3 Coaches to create long-term sustainability

This chapter introduces each of these four cornerstones of QCC. Throughout the book, you will learn how to develop and apply these concepts to not only improve your team's performance but your own as well.

Cornerstone 1 – Working "On" versus "In" the System

Time is extremely precious. What you do with your time has a direct impact on your personal success and the success of your team. If you begin to break down your typical week, you will discover that you literally make hundreds of decisions about the activities and people that will receive your time and energy. You must be purposeful in making these decisions to ensure you don't diminish your effectiveness. This doesn't happen by chance; it requires a conscious effort and continuous self-evaluation.

To be effective, you must continuously identify factors that affect the overall performance of your team. You must identify the obstacles that inhibit greater productivity. You need to understand what change or intervention will produce the greatest results. Managers often know the challenges their teams face, but it takes strategy and deliberate effort to develop and execute plans to overcome those obstacles.

Your role as the manager is to work "on" the system and create an environment that is conducive for your team's overall success. Examples of working "on" the system include the following activities:

- Performing QCC
- Creating and communicating a long-term vision
- Setting expectations and clarifying roles and responsibilities
- Analyzing current capabilities compared to customer needs
- Recruiting the right individuals for the team
- On-boarding new employees to the team
- Managing organizational change
- Creating effective employee development plans
- Developing product and process training
- Establishing stretch goals
- Staying current on industry trends

Although these activities are important, they often are not urgent. Many of the examples listed above do not involve quick fixes; they are not easy items to complete on a to-do list. Actions of this nature require deliberate thought and ongoing effort. Because of this, they are often neglected due to the pressing demands you face as a manager. You likely have good intentions at the start of the day, only to see those good intentions go down the drain as the day progresses and fires begin to ignite around you. Working "on" the system requires a planned and purposeful approach to improving strategic elements you can control. This takes discipline and focus.

While this sounds simple, it is one of the most challenging aspects of managing a team of people. Responding to urgent activities is easy and does not require forethought. Any manager can come to work in the morning without a plan and have her day filled with activities. The best managers are those who build their schedule around activities that involve working "on" the system.

Many people commonly identify time management as a significant challenge. Most of these individuals lose hours each day by working "in" the system; doing the work that their teams should be performing. Not only does this diminish the capacity to work on important issues, it also sets up employees to be dependent on their boss for routine activities. This is the ultimate scenario of how managers reduce their effectiveness.

Subsequent chapters will provide you with practical solutions to improve your effectiveness of working "on" the system.

Cornerstone 2 – Becoming a Level 3 Coach

Over the years our work has introduced us to thousands of leaders. Each is unique, possessing his or her own personal strengths and weaknesses. We've observed some leaders progress in their effectiveness, while others labored in a status quo reactionary environment where improvement was nearly impossible.

To keep things simple, we have grouped managers in one of three broad categories of effectiveness, with Level 3 Coaches being the highest level of effectiveness. It is important to note that the number of years of management experience is an insignificant factor in how an individual fits within our three levels. This insight tells us a few things.

- First, anyone regardless of experience can benefit from the basics of QCC.
- Second, old habits die hard. It's much easier to talk about improving than it is to actually commit to improving.
- Third, practicing QCC rapidly moves Level 1 Coaches to much higher performance and effectiveness levels.

Following is a breakdown of the three effectiveness levels:

LEVEL 1 COACHES *(Tell)*
• Tell people what to do and demonstrate poor listening skills
• Answer more questions than they ask
• Get bogged down in administrative work
• Manage to tasks and checklists
• Focus on outputs and react to results
• Operate under the assumption "I did it this way so you should do it this way"
• Manage individuals to the team average (Expanded in Chapter 9)
• Predominantly work "in" the system

LEVEL 2 COACHES *(Ask)*

- Demonstrate desired performance (move beyond "telling")
- Understand core team processes and systems
- Understand how process inputs impact process outputs
- Utilize QCC and demonstrate good listening skills
- Use data and reports to gather insight into individual performance
- Develop people to achieve results
- Periodically work "in" the system

LEVEL 3 COACHES *(Lead)*

- Assess individual employee strengths and weaknesses
- Focus on process inputs that drive key outputs
- Identify pipeline bottlenecks for each individual on the team
- Perform effective one-on-one coaching sessions
- Regularly practice QCC; demonstrate excellent listening skills
- Predominantly work "on" the system and spend time on strategic initiatives
- Coach the coach and develop QCC skills of other managers

Throughout the book, we will refer to the three levels with the goal of moving you to the highest level of coaching effectiveness.

Cornerstone 3 – Use Leverage to Create Greater Change

The more effectively you work "on" the system and apply the principles of QCC with your teams, the more capable your employees become. While this in and of itself is powerful, the benefits don't end there. The increase in individual capabilities of the team leads to something even more powerful for the manager: leverage.

Leverage strengthens your position. If you want to move a heavy object such as a large rock, but can't lift it, you can utilize a long metal pole to wedge or maneuver the rock. The pole allows you to create leverage, to strengthen your position, to achieve more power than you could do so otherwise in moving the rock.

You can achieve a similar result by using QCC. Instead of lifting a heavy object,

KEY CONCEPT

QCC = Increased Manager Leverage

you are strengthening your position by creating a higher performing team, thus allowing you to focus on more strategic activities.

Through QCC, you help your team members develop improved knowledge, skills and confidence, making them more independent and higher performing, ultimately increasing the overall effectiveness of the team. The benefit of this increased independence is your ability to stay above the fray and work "on" the system, focusing your attention on the critical activities that drive increased productivity. That is leverage at its finest. Too many managers lack this leverage and get bogged down in less important activities that are urgent and unplanned.

The Effective Coaching Model below illustrates a scenario in which you work "on" the system and utilize QCC. As coaching effectiveness improves and moves to the right, leverage increases. This improved leverage for you is realized in two distinct ways; less time spent reacting to urgent issues from your employees, and greater efficiency and production from your collective team.

The second Effective Coaching Model visually depicts what happens when you do not utilize QCC, and instead spend time working "in" the system doing the work of your team. As coaching effectiveness decreases and moves to the left, leverage is

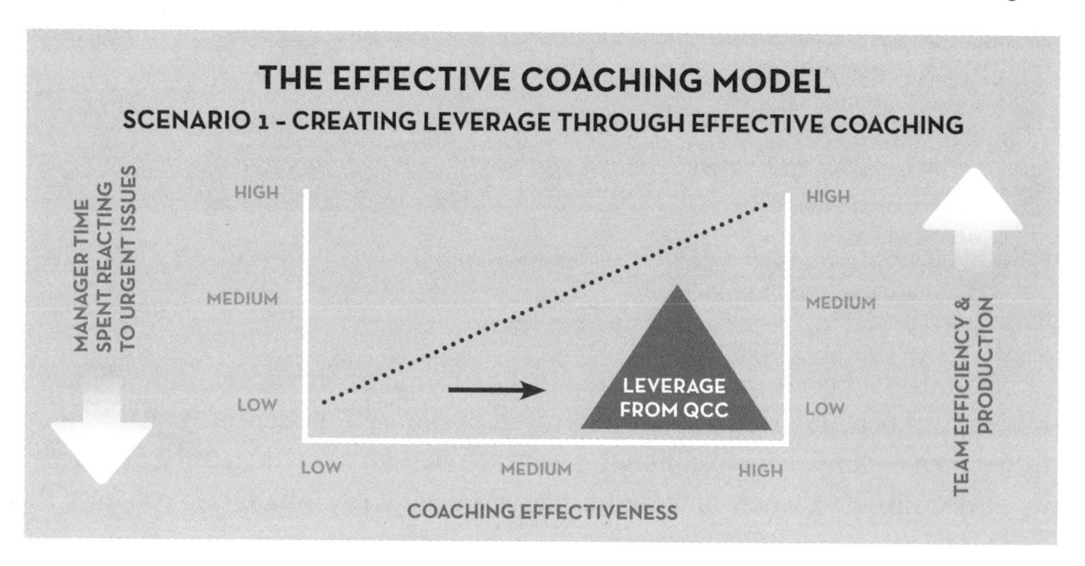

minimized. This diminished leverage is realized in two distinct ways by you; more time spent reacting to urgent issues from your employees, and lower efficiency and production from your collective team.

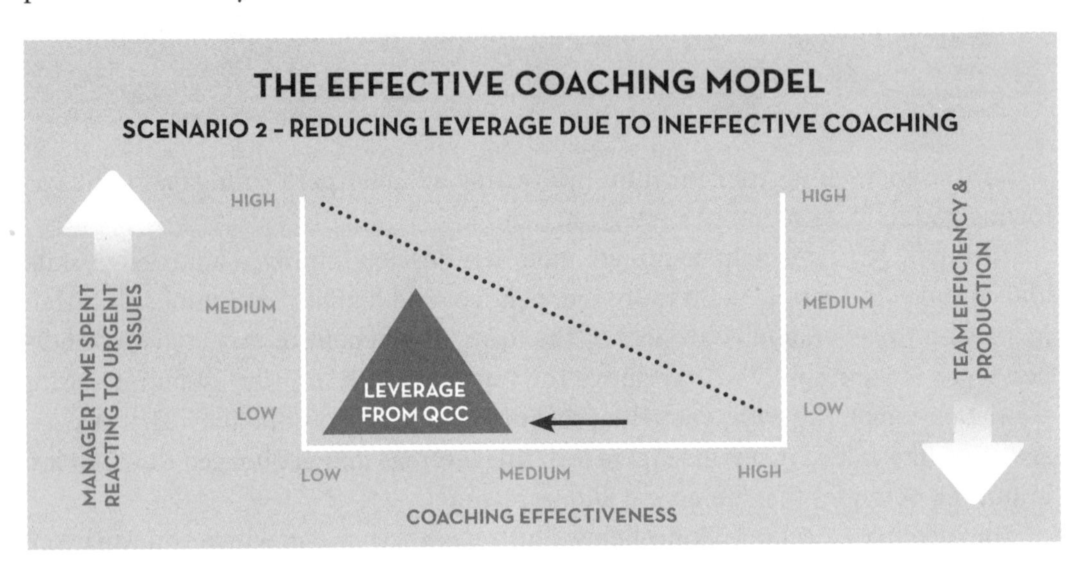

When QCC is properly applied, leverage manifests itself in multiple ways and you are able to create greater change and propel your team forward in ways previously unimaginable. Reducing the frequency in which you get pulled into urgent situations allows more time to proactively work "on" the system and spend time coaching your team. Your efforts will be rewarded in multiple ways as outlined in the following table:

TURBO-CHARGING INDIVIDUAL PERFORMANCE
1. People Producing Faster **2. Higher Engagement Levels** **3. Improved Retention**
TURBO-CHARGING TEAM PERFORMANCE
1. Increased Productivity **2. Greater System Insight** **3. Lower Management Expense**

Not only does coaching improve internal performance metrics as outlined previously, these benefits translate into improved customer experiences. Organizations facing increased market or economic pressures often focus on increasing productivity or decreasing expenses and ignore everything else. By using QCC, you have the tool set to simultaneously improve results in multiple areas.

Cornerstone 4 – Develop others to be Level 3 Coaches

Level 3 Coaches are high performing leaders that drive change and generate significant results through others. However, their greatest attributes are not just that they excel in working "on" the system and are highly skilled at QCC, but rather that they sustain long-term organizational performance by developing these same skills in other managers. Coaching the coach is truly what sets them apart from the rest of the population; they are able to pass on these attributes to other leaders and exponentially improve organizational performance.

The benefits of becoming proficient in the skills and activities of a Level 3 Coach are significant and will propel the results of your team. By harnessing the power of these Level 3 skills and attributes in other managers you improve organizational performance and ensure a sustained coaching culture.

At this point, you may still wonder if QCC is more efficient than just telling people what to do. After all, isn't that what our teams want us to do? To simply tell them what to do in "coaching sessions" so they can go back to their job and perform more effectively? The answer to this is a resounding "no." Asking teams and individuals targeted and strategic questions requires them to think through solutions and opens up possibilities that you have neither the time nor the firsthand knowledge to suggest. Telling someone what to do actually limits their performance, results, and sustainability of the direction you provide. At best, you will get one-time results that align to your directions.

While there are times when you give explicit directions to an employee, utilizing QCC will dramatically reduce these instances. Utilizing questions to develop an individual is one of the most powerful tools at the disposal of an effective coach. Unfortunately, questions are also one of the most underutilized tools used by most managers.

Many people in business have the perception that the further you ascend up the corporate ladder, the more you tell people what to do. One would assume that people are put in positions of authority to espouse their knowledge about how things need to be done, with the leader providing all of the answers. This thinking holds true in many organizations as well; when in charge, take charge. Doing otherwise is surely a sign of weakness or incompetence.

However, when this adage is challenged, you get little argument from people that asking questions and engaging in a dialogue is a much more effective way of developing people than simply "giving orders." Everyone has been at the receiving end of a one-sided conversation peppered with statements. Not only is this type of conversation less enjoyable, it is less effective at developing the critical capabilities targeted for development. We simply don't learn or retain information from this style. We learn by others asking thought-provoking questions that tap into our subconscious mind.

Many managers in today's high-pressure business environment don't take time to ask powerful questions or engage in meaningful dialogue with their team members. Our quick-fix society reinforces the mentality that it is easier to tell someone what to do versus exploring alternative solutions through effective questions. This not only creates less engaged employees, it also stifles innovation.

Asking effective questions is a learned skill; even the most direct person can adjust his approach with preparation, practice, and discipline. You have to make it a habit. Although not easy, it can be done, and the payoff is significant.

You will learn about the process of how to effectively harness the power of questions to create greater leverage. In addition, you will learn about other key concepts which will literally improve your performance overnight.

CLOSING THOUGHT

A common mantra for businesses is "our people are our greatest asset." This is a true statement for many organizations and goes beyond a marketing slogan. However, numerous managers leave a tremendous amount of human potential on the table, untapped and unfulfilled. This book will provide tactics to unlock the human potential utilizing the power of QCC.

Working "in" the system and increased leverage are mutually exclusive. Managers who work "on" the system recognize increased leverage across multiple areas at once. The end result is greater productivity and less time reacting to urgent issues.

CALL TO ACTION

- ❑ Review the activities you allocated time to this past week to determine whether they increased or decreased your leverage. What adjustment to those activities would increase your leverage? How would that leverage be recognized?
- ❑ Evaluate your management style against the criteria for Level 1, 2 and 3 Coaches. At what level do you currently operate? What habit(s) do you need to improve upon to ascend to the next Coaching Level?
- ❑ While conducting your next coaching session, mentally track the number of statements you make versus the questions you ask. Evaluate the ratio. What would the impact on the discussion be if you asked more questions?

Chapter 3
"On" vs. "In"

Time is one of the most precious resources available to you as a manager. The activities you choose to invest your time performing are a key factor in determining the level of success you achieve.

In chapter 2 we introduced the concept of working "on" versus "in" the system. Level 3 Coaches work "on" the system and create an environment that is conducive to the team's overall success. They utilize QCC to develop their team and continuously identify strategies to drive improvement, neither of which can be done if you are working "in" the system. The end result is improved capacity and independence for the team and increased time available for the manager; time which is invested in activities that drive even greater results.

Conversely, managers who work "in" the system perform activities in place of their team. If a report needs to be generated, they generate it. If a presentation needs to be created, they create it. Because they are busy executing activities for their team, these individuals don't have time to manage bigger picture issues and develop strategies to move the group forward.

Just so we're clear, working "in" the system is not the same as micromanagement. Individuals who micromanage keep their team on a short leash and don't allow them to work independently or have ownership in their role. However, they are still managing, albeit very ineffectively. Managers who work "in" the system aren't managing at all. They are busy performing the key activities for their teams.

Working "on" the system is a simple concept and one naturally assumes that managers spend their time in this space. Why in the world wouldn't they? There is so much to be gained by working "on" the system. Our work revealed this isn't the case. We frequently observed managers toiling away "in" the system performing work in place of their teams.

Why Managers Unintentionally Work "in" the System

So what causes this behavior? Why do you spend valuable time working "in" the system when so much can be gained by working "on" the system? We point to five common reasons:

1. **It is spontaneous and takes little planning.** As a 21st-century manager, you are extremely accessible to your team. Between e-mails, phone calls, instant messages, text messages or face-to-face conversations, employees can interrupt you at any time. Frequently employees pull you back "in" the system when they encounter challenges they are ill-equipped to solve. If you don't have a daily plan, you are susceptible to this situation and perpetuate the problem by fixing issues that are brought to your attention by employees. Your days are filled with "noise" when more important and strategic work is left sitting by the wayside.
2. **It appears to create immediate value.** Our culture is well steeped in instant gratification: fast food, Internet shopping, instant credit, and weight-loss programs are just a few examples. You often justify your worth by fixing problems for your employees. It is quick and effective, and you walk away feeling rewarded for your efforts.
3. **You enjoy doing so.** The tasks you are now managing others to complete are often the same activities you performed when in a previous role. Your ability to perform those activities well is likely a factor as to why you were promoted to lead a team. We all like to do what we do well, and it is appealing for you to go back and work "in" the system.
4. **Your ego gets in the way.** It is difficult to delegate tasks when you believe you are the most qualified to perform them. Subconsciously you believe your team can't execute the process as well as you, therefore you jump "in" the system and hijack the work to ensure the best outcome.
5. **You don't know what you don't know.** Organizations assume managers know more than they do, especially regarding to which activities are the most critical to perform in order to create sustainable productivity lift. There is little guidance for new and existing managers about the importance of creating leverage by working "on" the system and focusing on the key performance drivers within their control.

The process of working "on" the system is difficult and requires discipline. You frequently face situations in which the quickest path to resolution is to work "in" the system. Rather than invest time to coach people through new situations, you instead handle the issue yourself. Our field observations consistently validated this occurrence regardless of the function or discipline the manager worked.

For example, we witnessed call center managers make outgoing customer calls with members of their team. Instead of coaching the customer service representative prior to the call and having them lead the conversation, the manager took over and excluded the employee from the process. This left them on the outside looking in. The customer service issue was resolved, but at what expense? Was the employee better equipped to resolve the next issue in the absence of the manager? Not likely.

For the manager who has many demands on her time, this appears to provide the shortest path to resolution. Unfortunately, fast doesn't equal effective, as the personal capabilities of the customer service representative didn't improve, and they will struggle the next time they encounter a challenging situation.

A manager taking over a customer call does several things to reduce leverage. First, without an effective debrief following the call, the likelihood the employee recognizes the nuances of how the process was successfully executed are slim. Secondly, the customer might now look to the manager as the go-to person for future issues and will bypass the customer service representative.

Don't get us wrong. Having an employee observe a seasoned manager execute an effective phone call or process is vitally important. We are not opposed to this. What we are opposed to is when this is done without the intent to teach or transfer knowledge. Too often, managers demonstrate their prowess, but not in the context of a development opportunity. Coaching requires questions before and after the activity to review how and why the process moved down a certain path. Too often these pre- and post-conversations don't take place.

Our thinking around the importance of working "on" the system was challenged over the years. We originally believed working "on" the system was the key to success and the most important factor to create leverage and improve team productivity. However, after further examination, we discovered that working "on" the system, in and of itself, did not guarantee success.

This discovery was made as we observed managers who spent little to no time working "in" the system. They rarely performed activities for their team. They operated at a distance from the front line processes in their organization, in a command and control mode from the isolation and confines of their office. Rarely did they venture out and spend time with their teams and see firsthand what the team was experiencing.

According to our original thinking this must be good. Our position had always been if a manager didn't work "in" the system they must be working "on" the system. The goal was not to have managers perform work in place of their teams, and these managers clearly met that objective. However, there was one problem: these managers did not generate positive results. Their teams were not more productive or engaged. What was missing?

As we examined the situation, it became clear that working "in" the system and working "on" the system are not opposites. The absence of one does not ensure the presence of the other. Working "on" the system alone does not guarantee success.

KEY CONCEPT

Working "in" the system and working "on" the system are not opposites. The key to creating leverage is to work "on" the system and utilize QCC.

Working "on" the system without utilizing the tenets of QCC creates detached leaders who have little understanding or empathy of how or why their teams perform key activities. These are not the types of leaders organizations need. Organizations need leaders who possess insight into the challenges their teams face and the discipline to drive systemic change to improve performance.

We need to be careful here. We don't profess that you never work "in" the system. This is unrealistic, and not the goal. There are times when you must go deep into the system to learn about the challenges your team faces. Ultimately, this will increase your effectiveness. However, this must be a conscious and purposeful decision.

When and Why to Work "in" the System

We found three important situations which call for managers to temporarily work "in" the system.

KEY CONCEPT

It may be necessary for you to work "in" the system when:

1. *You Take a New Role*
2. *There is a Process, Product or Service Change*
3. *There is a Change in Market or Economic Conditions*

1. New Role - Moving into a new assignment is an exciting yet daunting task. In your career you may be fortunate to take on a variety of new roles and responsibilities. In today's economic climate, the grace period to learn your new role is compressed and you are expected to deliver quick results. You are expected to acclimate to your expanded responsibilities and immediately generate productivity improvements.

It is difficult to manage processes in which you are unfamiliar. Leadership skills are transferable across different departments, functions, companies, and industries. Examples are commonplace. What isn't transferable is the system insight or intimate knowledge of the processes for which you are now responsible.

In subsequent chapters, we elaborate on the power of gaining Greater System Insight or knowledge managers obtain via QCC. System Insight is the in-depth knowledge about people and processes for which managers are responsible. The likelihood of you leading a team to higher performance increases significantly when you are able to harness this powerful knowledge. It is a critical factor for success.

At the outset of a new job, the level of system insight you possess is often low. This is especially true if the new role involves an entirely new industry, business, or department. You have little experience to draw on to make educated decisions. Although strong leadership competencies provide immediate performance improvement, real change is realized as system insight is gained.

A means for you to remedy a lack of insight is to work "in" the system. Rolling up your sleeves and performing the activities your team performs. Specific activities are dependent on the type of team being led. An accounting manager might post debits and credits in the system, make collection calls to past-due customers, analyze budget trends, or perform the month-end close process. Managers gain a unique perspective by performing the work of their teams.

A sales manager might spend time in the field visiting customers, analyzing sales opportunities for a specific territory, understanding how company capabilities and products align with key clients, or preparing an agenda for a meeting with a large competitively held account.

There are several key points to clarify around this approach. It isn't random. It isn't by accident. The intent is to expeditiously expand system knowledge by targeting specific components of the system that require understanding. Secondly, it isn't indefinite. Once this knowledge is obtained, the goal must be to pull back out and work "on" the system. Too often managers go "in" but never come out.

KEY CONCEPT

The decision to work "in" the system is deliberate and planned.

Time working "in" the system should not be independent of the team. It is critical you work alongside individual performers and leverage the tenets of QCC. Doing so provides the dual benefit of learning about the process while gaining an understanding of the personal capabilities of each employee. Increased leverage!

We witnessed talented individuals take on new management assignments; some in roles in which they had system insight, and some not. Those without system insight dramatically increased their effectiveness by temporarily working "in" the system early in their time on the job. In addition to gaining knowledge, this activity created credibility and trust with the team. Building trust plays an important role when utilizing QCC. Upon achieving these objectives, these managers pulled back out of the system.

2. New Process, Product or Service – QCC requires you know the right types of questions to ask in different situations and frequently focuses on processes, products, and services. A significant change in any of these areas necessitates you temporarily work "in" the system to gain insight to clarify coaching opportunities and identify the right questions to ask.

In chapter 9, we introduce the bottleneck concept as a means to identify individual coaching opportunities with employees. You must possess adequate process knowledge to successfully identify where problems arise for each member of your team. Once identified, you utilize questions to develop employee skills and break the respective constraint. New or modified questions are often required when processes or products change.

The illustration below depicts a typical sales pipeline for a financial services company. Our purpose for referencing this pipeline example is to highlight how process changes require managers to temporarily work "in" the system to understand the implications to their coaching.

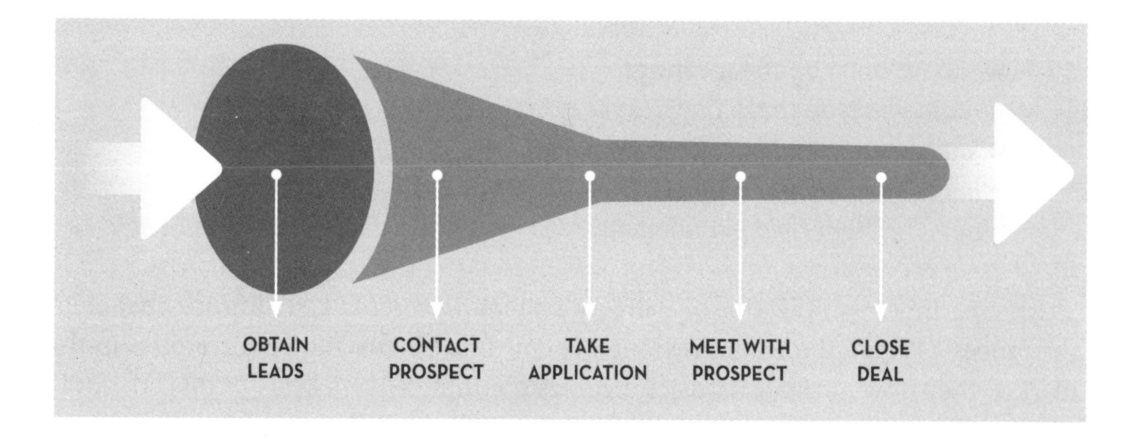

Let's assume you manage a team of eight individuals who perform this process. You receive a notice from the CEO stating a change to the first step of this process at the "Obtain Leads" step. The change involves moving away from sales people identifying and developing lead sources in their local market to a centralized lead delivery system. Historically, your team spent as much as 30% of their time performing this step prior to the change, so this represents a significant change in the process and how they will be expected to invest their time.

QCC Questions Used in the Old Process

Managers previously coached employees around identifying and building relationships with the best lead referral sources in the market. In this scenario, diagnostic questions they may have asked their employees included:

- Why are you targeting these lead referral sources?
  - ▹ *What attributes make them a good fit for our business model?*
  - ▹ *How do you know?*
  - ▹ *What percent of our lead needs are fulfilled from this source?*
  - ▹ *What alternatives do we have if we can't secure this relationship?*

- How do you plan to gain access to the decision makers?
  - ▹ *Will they be agreeable to meet with us?*
  - ▹ *If not, how can we leverage other relationships to provide a testimonial or endorsement on our behalf?*

- What do they like about their current partners?
  - ▹ *What are their frustrations?*
  - ▹ *What is the cost of those frustrations to their business?*
  - ▹ *Why would they shift their alliance and send their leads to us?*

- How do we open up the meeting?
  - ▹ *How do you plan to tell our story?*
  - ▹ *What is your initial benefits statement?*
  - ▹ *What is the potential impact of not doing this well?*
  - ▹ *What objections do you anticipate?*

Moving to a centralized lead delivery system represents a significant change in the process. Where the team previously spent time identifying opportunities in the market, they now navigate an electronic system that delivers leads to their desktop.

Whereas they previously had personal relationships with their lead referral sources and knew their customer demographics, they now operate using data and analytics, a very different process.

QCC Questions Used in the New Process

Diagnostic coaching questions in this scenario are different, and could include:

- Do you find certain leads more viable than others?
  - ▹ *What are the attributes of valuable leads?*
  - ▹ *Do you ask different questions for different lead attributes?*
  - ▹ *Do you use the same initial benefits statement with all leads?*
  - ▹ *Is it important to work the leads in the order they are provided?*
  - ▹ *What is the opportunity cost of not doing so?*

- Do you have enough leads to meet your production goals?
  - ▹ *How many leads can you effectively manage at one time?*
  - ▹ *Is there a better process in terms of how many leads you work?*
  - ▹ *What is the cost of not improving your pull through rate?*
  - ▹ *Do you have a follow-up system to ensure that you maximize the most valuable leads?*

The two sets of questions are very different. If you are the manager, how do you learn the impact of the process changes and get a handle on what these new questions are? The purpose of reviewing this scenario is not to dissect the new process; rather, it is to emphasize how changes require you to temporarily work "in" the system. This time and experience "in" the system allows you to identify the right types of questions to ask when coaching members of your team. Without taking time to sit alongside employees operating in this new process, your ability to effectively coach with questions is severely limited.

So what exactly does it mean to temporarily work "in" the system? It sounds fancy and theoretical, but it is quite simple. It means you get out of your office and perform the work that is typically performed by your team. It means gaining first-hand experience by executing key daily activities that are essential for employee success. It means understanding the capabilities, attributes, and knowledge required to successfully perform in the environment that you are managing.

In the example above, working "in" the system requires you to spend time navigating the screens in the new lead delivery system, personally working a lead, and understanding the attributes that make it successful or unsuccessful. The end goal of performing these activities is to identify the nuances of the new process that elicit success, and develop questions around those areas that you can use when performing QCC. One point worth reiterating; once you understand the impact to your team from the process changes, you need to pull out and go back to working "on" the system!

3. You must work "in" the system when there are significant changes to the market or economic conditions in which you operate – Economic cycles and changing market conditions come in many sizes and impact industries differently. The volatility in the financial services sector beginning in 2007 had a significant impact on the companies that operated in that segment. For example, the economic and mortgage crisis caused lenders to adjust sales practices, change product offerings, change underwriting and credit guidelines, and significantly reduce headcount. Some organizations went belly up while others held on by a string. Recipients of TARP (Troubled Asset Relief Program) money were under the microscope and faced intense public and government scrutiny. The one constant was that times had changed and it was no longer business as usual.

This is a radical example of changing market conditions, but what does it have to do with a manager needing to temporarily work "in" the system?

The issues facing a team following a market adjustment are different than those faced just a short while prior to the event. One moment the industry is producing record volume, and the next it has lost billions of dollars in market capitalization. The examples below highlight the challenges facing a leader in this situation:

- Old processes do not hold up to added regulatory scrutiny.
- Additional customer information is required to underwrite loans.
- Loan approval and fulfillment times take longer to complete.
- Quality measures and reporting packages need to be overhauled.
- Previous marketing strategies are no longer valid.
- Customer interactions are more contentious.
- Organizational changes are required to meet the new demands.

What makes this list daunting is not just the inexperience of the team in dealing with them; it is the inexperience of the manager in leading people through circumstances in which they have limited knowledge. It is difficult enough to develop people using QCC when you possess system insight and know the right questions to ask. It is nearly impossible to do so when you don't possess this insight or know the right questions to ask! If you have worked for a manager in that situation, you understand the associated frustrations.

This situation calls for a manager to temporarily work "in" the system to experience the challenges firsthand and understand the elements to succeed in the altered environment. Without this knowledge, the manager's ability to coach is diminished.

The market condition changes experienced in the financial sector were monumental. The point of using this example was out of familiarity; everyone has knowledge of its occurrence because it was in the news on a daily basis. Don't confuse the scope of this example as being the measuring stick for changing conditions in your respective industry. Smaller changes can necessitate temporarily working "in" the system.

Working "in" the system has it's time and place as outlined on the previous pages. However, to effectively deploy QCC, it is critical managers do so in a purposeful manner, on a temporary basis, and with specific objectives.

Your role of the manager is to work "on" the system and create an environment that is conducive to your team's overall success. This requires a conscious effort and continuous self-evaluation. "On" system activities require devoted time and can't be pushed aside for more urgent issues. In subsequent chapters, we delve into strategies to ensure you make them a priority and keep them on your calendar.

CLOSING THOUGHT

Working "on" the system is a critical success factor for Level 2 Coaches. You cannot afford to spend precious time working "in" the system performing activities for your team. As a manager, your job is to create leverage by developing the skills of your team and facilitating the development of solutions that collectively move the group forward.

There are appropriate times for you to work "in" the system. However, decisions to work "in" the system must be deliberate and temporary versus reactive and permanent. The goal is to temporarily go "in" to gain knowledge and then come back out.

Working "on" the system must be accompanied by QCC; doing otherwise creates detached leaders that don't understand the challenges their teams face.

CALL TO ACTION

- ❏ Review the key activities you performed over the past two weeks. Determine how many hours you devoted to each activity.
- ❏ Categorize the activities as either working "on" the system or "in" the system. Calculate the percentage of total time you spent working "on" the system versus working "in" the system. Is this the appropriate balance to maximize the performance of your team? Why or why not?
- ❏ Prospectively, what key activities do you plan to perform over the next two weeks? What is your time allocation of "on" system activities versus "in" system activities? Is this the appropriate balance to maximize the performance of your team? Why or why not?
- ❏ If performed over the next 30 to 60 days, what "on" system activity would significantly improve your position of leverage?

Chapter 4
Coaching vs. Managing

When you walk into a bookstore you can find shelf after shelf of books on leadership. In fact, you can find a few on coaching as well. However, books on management don't seem to be as popular or perhaps are a little out of vogue. Does that mean that management and the process of managing are unimportant? Does managing no longer matter? We get the sense that some of these books should be entitled "Let's Abandon Management."

Although this book focuses on understanding the power of coaching as well as practicing and improving your coaching skills, this should not come at the expense of proper management thinking and techniques. Too often, management and coaching gets tangled up, and the two become interchangeable terms.

Business professionals need to understand both coaching and managing and effortlessly switch gears between the two. We coach and we manage; many times all within the same day and maybe within the same conversation.

Coaching vs. Managing

So what is management, and how is it different from coaching?

Managing is about the "what." Managing has a lot to do with organizing, planning, directing, and controlling. At its core, managing is about allocating resources and directing these resources in a way that accomplishes the goals of the organization in the most efficient and effective way. Key activities include planning, organizing, budgeting, and supervising activities. Managers review and interpret data, understand qualitative changes in their organization, and make adjustments to their plans and resource allocations. This is really important stuff. It is hard to be a top tier coach if you are a terrible manager.

Coaching is about the "how." While good management is essential, great coaching can take performance to a higher level. Certainly, there is a time for very directive action with people. Most managers need to use this type of approach from time to time.

When it's necessary, it's necessary. However, the performance leap within a team occurs when people willfully commit and understand how to perform. It occurs when a coach asks the right questions in the right way to create higher levels of engagement. By answering these questions, it becomes obvious to the person how they should behave and perform to reach new levels.

Managing is important. In fact, it's important that you are a good manager. But don't confuse managing with coaching. If you manage people, you take on the responsibility for controlling them. Our experience is that you will generate significantly more lift by managing materials and reports while making time to coach people.

Here is another way to look at it: management is the oil in the gears that keeps the engine lubricated. Without oil, the engine seizes up. But it's coaching that harnesses all the performance from the engine.

The chart below illustrates several key differences between managing and coaching.

MANAGING	COACHING
Focused on resources and materials	Focused on people
Output driven	Input driven
Controlling	Choice
Authority	Buy-in
Resolves issues	Develops people
Directive	Collaborative
Owned by manager	Owned by employee
E-mail or group meetings	One-on-one conversations
About the result	About the person
Statement based	Question-Centric

In summary, being a good manager creates the foundation for being an excellent coach and leader. Now that we have a framework for understanding "management," we can proceed to coaching.

The term *coaching* is commonly tossed about in corporate America. Over recent years, an influx of specialists have dissected every aspect of coaching: sales coaching, leadership coaching, executive coaching, presentation coaching, and even wardrobe coaching.

This abundance of consultants has not helped organizations understand how to define and execute effective performance coaching with simple practicality. Businesses are certainly familiar with the term, but they are no better equipped to help their teams understand what coaching is, or more importantly, how to develop the necessary skills to perform it at a consistently high level.

On the surface, coaching appears to be simple and straightforward. Many executives assume their managers are competent in this area and leave it at that. They don't take time to dig in and better understand the fundamental elements of effective coaching, or how their manager's capabilities align with these key criteria.

When we ask senior team leaders how effective their frontline managers are at coaching their teams, the majority respond "great" or "very good." Rarely is the response "poor" or "not good enough." Taken at face value, these responses indicate little opportunity for improvement. Everyone appears to be coaching at a high level. However, this is one area where organizations can't afford to take things at face value.

So what is the best means to assess the coaching ability of a manager? Sometimes it is obvious based on performance and behaviors, but not always. Below is a simple Two-Step Closed Loop Model to follow in order to assess the coaching ability of a manager.

Ask – The first step to assess the coaching ability of a manager is to ask the individual a series of questions; questions that dig below the surface and uncover the reality of the situation. This is vital. We have yet to meet a manager who didn't answer "yes" to superficial questions in reference to whether they believe in coaching or consistently coach their team. Who wouldn't answer those types of questions positively? It is not until more probing questions are asked that one can adequately assess true coaching effectiveness. In the next chapter, we will provide additional information involving the strategic use of such questions.

Observe – The second step is to actively observe a manager coach. This is absolutely critical. There is no substitute for watching someone in action, observing their approach and gauging the response of the person being coached. Observation provides the truest measure of coaching effectiveness. Even the worst coaches can respond to generic inquiry with convincing and politically correct answers. However, executing an effective coaching conversation is more difficult to fake your way through. The power of this two-step process comes from combining questions with observation.

Senior managers aren't intentionally deceptive when it comes to evaluating the coaching abilities of their managers. They simply assume too much about the presence and quality of these skills. They often give managers the benefit of the doubt because they achieve good results. They falsely conclude good managers are automatically good coaches. Our work with a large geographically dispersed sales organization provides a good illustration of this scenario.

A Personal Experience – The Manager Who Assumed Too Much

During a particular engagement, we conducted field visits to numerous regions across North America. The purpose of the visits was to understand how the agreed upon coaching strategy was being executed in the field and how it could be improved from the original model.

One particular trip began by having lunch with an area manager who was responsible for multiple retail locations. Our conversation focused on the store we were scheduled to visit that afternoon; the strengths of the manager, the specific needs of the employees, and the overall performance of the team. Over the course of the conversation, we asked the area manager how they rated the coaching skills of the store manager. His response was "great." The area manager continued by stating, "This is a veteran manager with years of experience and is one of the best coaches we have in the area."

After entering the store and exchanging pleasantries, the first priority was to spend time with the store manager so that he and the area manager could put together their game plan for the visit. Upon establishing the game plan, the next activity included the area manager observing the store manager execute a one-on-one coaching session with a salesperson.

The area manager and store manager prepared for the coaching session and both agreed that this particular salesperson struggled at the front end of the sales process. The salesperson talked to a lot of prospects, actually the most in the store, but was unable to advance the majority of those conversations into viable opportunities because they couldn't get the prospect to come into the store for a face-to-face visit. According to the store manager, the salesperson had a lot of natural talent and was progressing nicely in her development.

Customers who did agree to meet with the salesperson face-to-face frequently ended up purchasing a product. The problem was that the salesperson didn't schedule enough face-to-face customer meetings to be successful.

After agreeing to the focus of the session, we all sat down with the sales- person for the coaching conversation. Several things quickly became apparent from our observations. First, the coaching skills of the store manager were poor at best. Instead of asking questions to engage the employee, the manager endlessly lectured the salesperson on what she needed to do. The discussion was scattered across different elements of the sales process instead of being focused on the specific area of need with which the salesperson was struggling. Nothing was written down, and no specific action items were agreed to. By the end of the session, the salesperson was downtrodden and exhausted. The session was a classic example of someone dictating with statements instead of coaching.

The second thing that became apparent was this was the first formal conversation that the manager had conducted with the salesperson in nearly four months. This salesperson was starving for attention and development; yet little time had been invested in the fundamentals of selling or how to articulate a compelling value proposition to the customer.

Following the session, I asked the area manager whether his assessment of the store manager's coaching skills had changed since our lunch discussion. His response was a resounding "yes." The area manager was shocked about how ineffective the coaching session was and how poor the manager's coaching skills were. In the words of the area manager, "I grossly overestimated how good the store manager was in regard to coaching." The manager had made assumptions but never confirmed them through effective questions or observation. The coaching skills that were earlier described as "excellent" were far from that. Subsequent conversations with the area manager surfaced an even bigger concern: whether the coaching skills of other store managers in their organization were as good as they had originally assumed.

Let's evaluate the previous store manager example by referring back to the differences between managing and coaching outlined in the table presented earlier in this chapter. A comparison of the attributes from both lists illustrates why this scenario is an example of 'Managing' and not 'Coaching.' A few notable attributes include the following:

- The manager controlled the conversation with statements and did little to engage the employee in the process; the employee had little choice but to accept what she was told. It was not a collaborative process.
- All potential solutions or actions were owned by the manager and not the employee.
- The conversation focused on achieving results and not understanding the needs and challenges the individual faced in achieving those results. It was not about developing the employee and her personal style.

The previous example was not an isolated situation. There were many others, each slightly different, but tied together by a common thread. Organizations focus little on developing practical performance coaching skills necessary for today's managers. Managers fortunate enough to work for a progressive leader may learn the tricks of the trade directly from firsthand experience. They are the recipient of excellent coaching and often emulate those same strategies. Those less fortunate are left fending for themselves; learning under fire through a process of trial and error. This process is costly to the organization and frustrating to the people wanting to be developed.

Unfortunately, available training often misses the mark. It focuses more on the mechanics of how to manage a team versus how to coach a team. The area of reporting is a good illustration of this scenario. Managers are exposed to reports measuring performance, yet little time is spent developing the skills and practices necessary to coach the employees that these reports identify as underperforming.

The assumption is that managers are equipped to figure this out on their own, which is simply not true. This issue has nothing to do with intelligence, desire or talent. Rather, it has everything to do with a learned skill that receives minimal focus, time or attention in most organizations.

Organizations that offer training on the topic of coaching often introduce a standard coaching model. This is certainly a step in the right direction, but such training is only the first step and must be followed with consistent reinforcement through QCC. A key difference between training and coaching is that training focuses on the acquisition of knowledge, and coaching focuses on the application of knowledge. They are hopelessly intertwined. For example, it is unrealistic to believe that a new employee can receive classroom training and effectively go back to his job and be productive without effective coaching and reinforcement from his manager.

Managers perceive coaching as an activity performed only when time permits. It is an afterthought. This is wrong. Coaching is a primary responsibility, and less im-

KEY CONCEPT

QCC Develops Critical Thinking Skills of Employees

portant functions should be scheduled around time allocated to coaching. It needs to come first, not last. This requires a paradigm shift for many managers.

Effective coaches utilize the power of QCC to develop the critical thinking skills of their team. Managers frequently break this tenet by telling instead of asking. The use of questions is essential in getting an employee to mentally develop his critical thinking and reach his own conclusions. This is much different than telling someone what to do. Much of this book focuses on improving these critical skills.

CLOSING THOUGHT

Management is important, and effective management is the gateway to coaching. We do not endorse that managers spend 100% of their time coaching. There are times when a manager needs to manage, and coaching would be inappropriate based on the situation and/or the individual.

There are distinct differences between coaching and managing. These differences must be understood. Managers must understand when one is more appropriate than the other. They are not interchangeable and serve different purposes.

The Two-Step Closed Loop Model is the most effective means to assess the coaching capabilities of a manager. This process combines asking questions with observation. Too often leaders assume their managers are good coaches because they produce good results or are able to provide adequate answers about how they coach others. Observation allows a leader to quickly determine the true effectiveness of a manager's coaching competence.

Good coaches recognize the power of QCC and understand how it is utilized to develop the critical thinking skills of their team. Rather than lecture solutions to their employees, they instead choose to ask thought-provoking questions.

CALL TO ACTION

- ❑ Referencing the table presented in this chapter that distinguishes the differences between coaching and managing, assess the next one-on-one meeting you have with an employee and evaluate whether you do more coaching or managing.
- ❑ What attributes from the list, if improved, would yield the most significant impact on your coaching effectiveness? (e.g. Asking more questions, increasing collaboration and buy-in from the employee, focusing on developing the individual instead of focusing only on desired results, etc.)
- ❑ Use the Two-Step Closed Loop Model to evaluate the coaching effectiveness of your managers. Prior to the coaching session, ask them questions about what their objectives are for the session. Follow this up by observing the session and providing feedback on how they executed against their plan.

Chapter 5
Core Elements of QCC

Establishing clarity around the core elements of QCC is imperative to successfully implement a coaching discipline in any organization. People need to speak the same language in order to have a consistent understanding of coaching fundamentals.

This chapter introduces and explores five core elements of QCC.

KEY CONCEPT

Core Elements of QCC

1. *Consistent Coaching Process*
2. *Predictable Frequency*
3. *Relevant Coaching Topics*
4. *Coach to Inputs and not Results*
5. *Mutually Agreed-Upon Goals*

1. Consistent Coaching Process

Individuals who manage employees using a traditional management approach will find themselves operating out of their comfort zone as they transition to QCC. Using a question-centric approach requires different skills, habits and behaviors. New habits require practice and repetition until they become engrained and part of a standard routine. In the meantime, as habits are being formed it is important to have a defined roadmap to reference and keep you on track.

Think about a situation in which you got lost or turned around and you had no idea which direction was which. Maybe you were on a hike in the mountains, driving on a country road, or simply lost in a big city. It is a paralyzing feeling when you are unable to establish your bearings and determine the proper direction to travel. Without GPS, a map or a key landmark to reference, you are in for a challenging and frustrating situation. However, having any one of those three tools will dramatically improve your outlook by providing you with the direction you need to proceed to safety.

A similar feeling of helplessness occurs when navigating through coaching conversations early in your transition to QCC. To minimize the probability of you losing your way when coaching employees, we developed the Coaching Conversation Process to act as your map and keep you on course.

Coaching Conversation Process

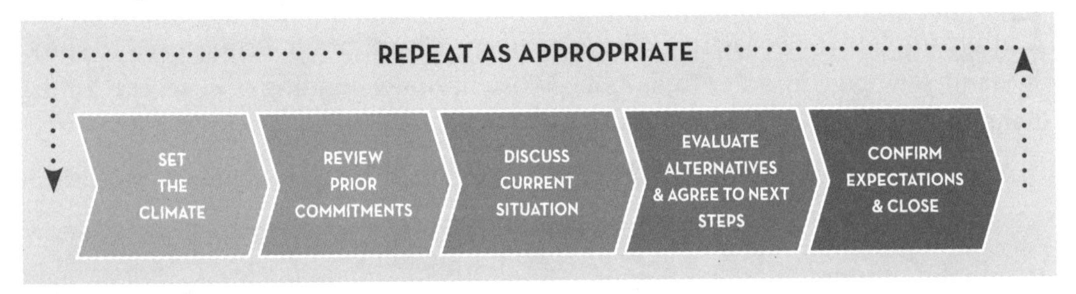

As you can see, the Coaching Conversation Process is not overly complicated. It is an extremely simple model. However, don't confuse the simplicity of the process with the significant leverage that can be generated from its use. It is simple, but not simplistic. Too often managers look for a silver bullet or quick fix to improve the performance of their teams. Our experience suggests the surest path to greatness is achieved by executing fundamental processes extremely well.

The content and focus of a coaching discussion is ever-changing, but the conversation is repeatable from a process perspective.

The following section outlines the key objectives that fall under each step of the process. The Coaching Conversation Process is not intended to limit or script the conversation, but instead to keep you on task and provide directional support when coaching others. Subsequent chapters will overlay additional elements to bring the Coaching Conversation Process to life. This includes specific questions that can be used in each step to engage the hearts and minds of those you are coaching.

The benefits of the Coaching Conversation Process are not reserved for only you as the coach, as this consistent protocol creates an environment where employees know what to expect when they meet with you. Without this structure, many employees are left guessing as to what the real agenda might be. We witnessed managers who intentionally made things unpredictable in an attempt to keep everyone on "edge" and elevate performance. This approach has the opposite effect as it creates mistrust and is an inefficient use of time, neither of which can be afforded in today's challenging environment.

When you get below the surface, disgruntled employees are often exasperated by the unpredictability of their manager. Unpredictability wears people down and has a direct impact on morale and turnover. Managers exhibit this unpredictability with their teams in different ways: scattered focus and points of emphasis, changing goals and strategies, varying intent, and ever-changing emotional tone and style are several examples. Anyone who has worked for a manager that exhibits unpredictability knows how difficult this variable is to anticipate. One day you get scolded, and the next day you are praised. Both results had little to do with you, and more to do with external factors that led to the inconsistency of your manager. When managers do not execute coaching fundamentals, their approach takes a toll on productivity and engagement of the team.

The sub-objectives for each step of the Coaching Conversation Process are outlined below.

Step 1 – Set The Climate
- Build rapport and establish trust
- Strengthen the relationship with the person you are coaching
- Review the agenda and establish expectations for your time together

Step 2 – Review Prior Commitments
- Employee recap of the agreed upon decisions and actions from the last coaching session
- Align expectations

Step 3 – Discuss Current Situation
- Evaluate the impact of the action taken
- Review progress and improvement against the goal
- Determine if additional improvement is required

Step 4 – Evaluate Alternatives and Agree to Next Steps
- Brainstorm options
- Review potential obstacles and risks
- Select the best option and next steps

Step 5 – Confirm Expectations and Close
- Employee recap of discussion
- Review accountabilities and expectations
- Confirm time to reconnect

The goal of Step 1 is to establish a solid foundation from which to conduct your coaching session(s). The intent of Step 1 is to establish rapport, build trust and develop a productive relationship with an employee. Early in a coaching relationship this includes talking about expectations of your time together, understanding how the person you are coaching best learns, what their natural talents are and how frequently you need to meet. In addition to work-related discussions, Step 1 involves asking questions about things outside of work including hobbies and other areas of personal interest.

A surprising theme that we consistently uncovered in our coaching observation work was how frequently Step 2 (Review Prior Commitments) was skipped by the manager. In fact, our findings revealed that conducting a review of previous commitments occurred in less than 20% of coaching sessions observed. This step is imperative in creating behavior changes with your employees and, if left undone, undermines the essence of your coaching efforts.

Instead of following up on prior commitments, too many managers immediately focus on new issues requiring attention. This reduces the likelihood that employee behavior will change. Beyond the short-term setback of not fulfilling agreed-upon commitments, the long-term effectiveness of future coaching sessions is greatly diminished. It doesn't take long for an employee to recognize there are no repercussions if they choose not to execute their action plan.

In light of all the challenges you face as a manager –meetings, emails, and constant interruptions – you develop bad habits regarding the follow-up you do with your employees. Correcting these habits by becoming more disciplined is a powerful step in the Coaching Conversation Process. When your employees know they will be asked to report on their actions following the last meeting, they will execute on their accountabilities and enter the coaching session prepared to discuss the associated outcomes. In subsequent chapters we provide you with simple questions to ensure effective follow-up.

2. Predictable Frequency

QCC must be predictable in terms of the frequency in which it is performed as predictability is a powerful means to change behavior and form new habits. Whether weekly, bi-weekly or monthly is dependent on the needs and situations of each employee. It is important to recognize that those needs will change over time. Regardless of the interval, the person being coached knows that time is allocated to them on a recurring basis.

In the previous chapter, the case study described a situation in which we observed a store manager coach an employee. As a result of this process, we learned this was the first coaching session that had taken place in four months. Think about the unstated message this action communicates to the employee. For starters, it indicates their development is not a priority for their manager, and if they are going to be successful, they better figure out a way to do it on their own.

Our work has shown positive results when managers establish a predictable frequency of coaching. Confidence increases when an employee knows his manager consistently allocates time with them to focus on skills and personal development.

Coaching is an ongoing process and not just a one-time event. The frequency, focus, and intensity of coaching will vary over time, but it doesn't stop. This includes working with top performers. Everyone has opportunities to improve, and your role as a manager is to utilize QCC to tap into the inner potential of each individual. Just because a person on your team doesn't have glaring opportunities for improvement doesn't mean her performance can't be improved by coaching to her strengths. A good coach understands this.

Anytime we engage with a new group, the leader is excited about our process but nervous about how their veteran team members will react to a different way of doing things. They are unsure about their willingness to learn something new or improve a skill that could lift performance.

Our approach with these folks has been to meet with them ahead of time so they are not surprised by the strategy. We explain our method, answer questions, and put no pressure on them to adapt to our approach as they "probably already know this stuff." While our engagements have demonstrated time and time again that the veterans don't actually "know this stuff," it does take some pressure off and allows them to absorb without the need to demonstrate they are "smarter" than the rest of the team.

Interestingly enough, these same individuals consistently turn out to be the biggest champions of our coaching process. Veterans can and will learn if the right positioning is provided. QCC is a tool that elevates performance to the next level for all parties, and most top performers understand that improvement never ends.

3. Relevant Coaching Topics

Unlike most training, QCC focuses on real organizational issues encountered by employees. The stronger the relevance and connectedness to day-to-day processes and results, the more powerful QCC becomes. It is about developing skills and strategies to resolve issues and achieve greater results. Coaching is not providing informational updates to your team.

We have witnessed hundreds of coaching sessions, some more effective than others. A key success factor distinguishing the more effective sessions is the ability of the manager to connect coaching to relevant daily activities the employee performs as part of his job. Rather than conducting a session where the goal of the manager is to fire up an employee, good coaching gives people the tools and plan that they can apply to their day-to-day work, resulting in measurable improvement. Without this, most people quickly revert to old habits. By integrating coaching with an individual's role and daily activities, you help your team build and sustain performance.

By asking the right questions at the right time about real situations, you focus your employee's efforts on the activities that maximize performance. Employees are more likely to pay attention to your coaching when the outcome will put money in their pocket through improved performance ratings or hitting incentive compensation goals. The key for you is to connect the conversation to activities and goals by which you measure the performance of your team.

Ineffective coaching conversations focus on generalities and don't target specific behavior changes or skill improvement. In these situations, managers tell employees what to do and use language that is vague and theoretical. For example, telling employees things like:

- You need to spend time on the right activities.
- Make sure to ask better questions.
- You have to become a better listener.
- It is important to build strong relationships.
- Be strategic and consultative in your approach.

Granted those are good objectives, but telling someone to do them doesn't improve the probability for successful execution. You are essentially reiterating the obvious. This is nothing more than unapplied theory and results in frustrated employees.

To be effective, you need to have specific discussions around real opportunities. For example, instead of telling a person to "be strategic," ask questions such as the following:

- What is the goal with this specific initiative?
- Who are the key stakeholders?
- What types of objections will those stakeholders have?
- Who are the influencers?
- Who should you gain support from first?
- How can this be accomplished?
- What information can be shared with these individuals?
- What are the potential next steps?

Every situation calls for questions tailored to discover, discuss, and implement opportunities for improvement. Simply telling someone to be strategic is not coaching!

Do you see the difference in the two approaches? The latter represents a conversation that is not generic. It focuses on real opportunities and how to advance them in the process. It targets behaviors and strategies that, if executed, result in tangible progress. It applies classroom training to activities relevant to success. It builds capacity by developing critical thinking skills through the use of QCC.

4. Coach to Inputs and Not Results

Previously we clarified the differences between managing and coaching. Management focuses on results, where QCC focuses on changing behaviors to improve results. Attention must be focused on continuously evaluating strategies, tactics, and behaviors that lead to achieving desired objectives. It is impossible to coach things that have already occurred. What's happened has happened. Coaching proactively focuses on process inputs, not reactively discussing process results. When coaching others, you must focus on the left side of the process diagram below. Your role is to help employees understand the process inputs that have a correlation to the process results.

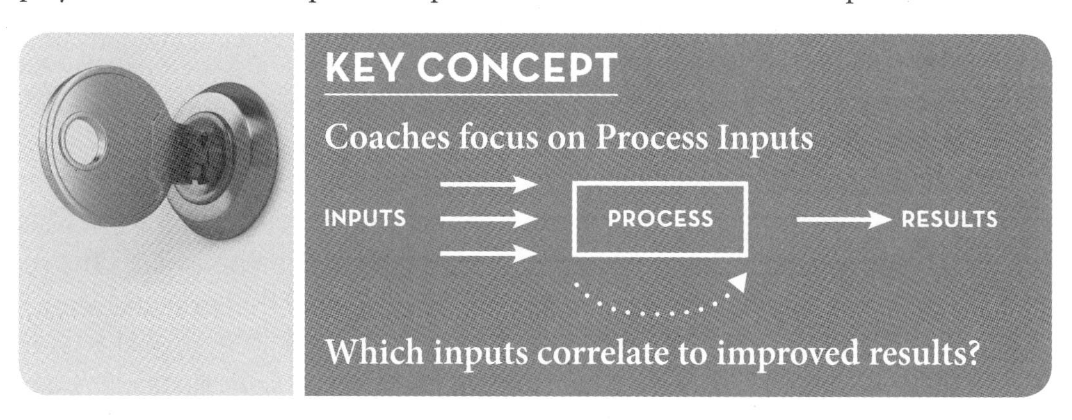

This doesn't imply that results don't matter; people are paid upon results. We get it. We expect it of ourselves and for those that work for us. However, asking someone to double their results for the week is not the way to get there. If they knew how to do this, don't you think they would already be doing it? It's the same as telling a gymnast not to fall off the balance beam or a baseball player not to let a ground ball go between his legs. The gymnast, baseball player and employee all desire good results; if they don't, you have a much bigger issue. Coaching is about "how" to do something and is input-driven. It is not a post-commentary on a less-than-satisfactory performance. Effective coaches understand this. Poor managers do not.

Let's break down the previous diagram with specific inputs and outputs to illustrate this important concept.

Examples of traditional sales results include: units sold, total revenue, gross profit, or average sale amount. Picture these on the right-hand side of the process diagram. Now focus on the left-hand side of the process diagram and identify activities or inputs that drive these desired results. These are things that a sales manager needs to focus on to drive improved results. These activities include territory assessments to maximize sales opportunities, blocking time in the day to prospect new clients, executing weekly communication plans with existing customers, or creating detailed customer call plans for upcoming appointments. Effective coaches ask questions around the planning, execution and performance of these and other key inputs.

Too often, managers assume too much when it comes to the skills of their team. Just because a salesperson is confident and has an outgoing, likeable personality doesn't mean that he can navigate a conversation with a savvy client. It takes more than personality to be successful. Good managers spend time on the left side of the process, providing coaching around the inputs that are critical to achieving successful results. This is done through QCC and followed up with observation.

Following is a case study that further illustrates the importance of coaching to the input side of the process model.

A Personal Experience – Coaching to Process Inputs

An individual, let's call her Jane, requested time with me to discuss the results from a 360-degree leadership assessment (a tool that provides anonymous feedback from managers, employees and peers.) Although she fared well in many areas, Jane received critical feedback in several specific competencies. The message was loud and clear. Further advancement opportunities in the organization were limited unless these specific competencies were improved.

People tend to react differently to 360-degree feedback. Some brush it off as irrelevant. Some get angry and defensive. Some deny it completely. They assume others are out to get them with their comments. Although Jane didn't elaborate on her initial reactions, she had since taken the feedback to heart and came to me seeking guidance on how to improve.

Although Jane was widely recognized as a person with great drive, passion, and an ability to achieve results, she also was a leader that left bodies in her wake. At the conclusion of projects, her superiors, peers and subordinates weren't enamored with the idea of working with Jane in the future. They didn't care for her style. They felt like Jane was arrogant and more concerned about individual recognition and taking credit for the team. Jane would challenge others to meet deadlines by dropping names of executives that she needed to report results to in upcoming meetings. Not exactly a means of motivating and inspiring others to greatness. Unfortunately, Jane had a well-established negative personal brand.

Jane was looking for help in how to change her brand. She was open to suggestions, but unsure of where to start. I sketched the process diagram below, specifying the key themes from her 360 degree assessment.

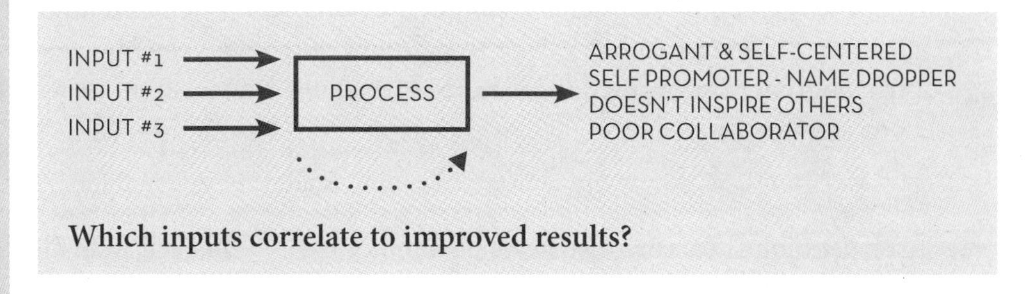

Which inputs correlate to improved results?

How do you coach a person like Jane? Do you simply tell her to be less arrogant and work hard to inspire others? Seems logical, but it isn't very helpful. Telling someone to be less arrogant simply states the obvious; telling Jane to do something that she is at a loss for how to do.

Instead, the coaching opportunity lies on the input side of the process, where changing specific behaviors leads to improved results. I asked Jane lots of questions, helping her think through past situations and behaviors. A few of the questions were:

- *Tell me about how people perceive you? Why have some people come to this conclusion? How might your actions lead them to this conclusion? Can you think of specific situations that might have given them this impression?*

- *Has building relationships with project partners outside of the formal meetings been important to you? If yes, describe how you go about doing this. If not, tell me how you might go about building relationships outside of meetings?*

- *What do you seek to understand regarding your partner's thoughts and perspective about the project you are embarking on together? How does this process personally affect them, their success and their goals?*

- *How do you learn about your partner's style, motivation, and strengths? Do you ask questions? Who does most of the talking? How might these things influence their perceptions about you?*

- *Describe how you present yourself? How do you introduce yourself? How do you position your role in the project? What kinds of words do you use?*

While not an exhaustive list, these questions target the input side of the process. Through this process, Jane came to several significant conclusions about why people reached certain perceptions about her, and how minor changes in her approach may lead to different outcomes. The questions simply guided her down the path. Chapter 7 explores more about using questions in this manner.

A manager's job is to assess where opportunities exist and coach individuals to success. Future chapters provide a strategy to identify where in the process a manager should focus her coaching efforts.

5. Mutually Agreed-Upon Goals

The fifth core component of QCC is to develop mutually agreed-upon goals between you and the person being coached.

Coaching is not a means for you to force your agenda on an employee; nor is it an opportunity for an employee to focus on areas that are not relevant to improving performance and delivering results in key areas. It is essential that you and your employee mutually agree on specific goals and actions at the conclusion of a coaching session.

Managers often assume their role is to have all the answers all the time, operating under the premise that their primary responsibility is to tell people what to do. Managers operating with this mentality believe their role is to push actions on to an employee without achieving buy-in. The manager comes into the meeting knowing that there is a problem with a certain part of the process. Rather than ask questions of the employee to gain his perspective on why this breakdown occurs, the manager jumps to solutions based on past experience. It is the old ready-fire-aim. Fast, yes; effective, no.

Individuals adhering to this principal fail to realize these actions minimize their ability to create leverage and generate innovative solutions to problems. Coaching is a dialogue, not a monologue. It's not about lecturing someone. The road to success is long and bumpy when managers spend their days telling people what to do and how to do it.

To be an effective coach, you must ask relevant questions related to the current responsibilities of your employee; questions that challenge her thinking and help her evaluate opportunities and challenges ahead. By using the tenets of QCC, you and your employee pull together to form solutions in which the employee takes accountability and ownership.

Recently we discussed the idea of push versus pull with a friend who is a medical doctor. We found it interesting that he quickly agreed. He referenced patients that needed to lose weight. "It's fast and easy to order them to lose the necessary weight, but at next year's physical we end up with the same weight issue. I find that if I engage my patient in a conversation and ask them the right questions, they take more ownership in the solution and tend to keep the weight off."

In fact, it's our experience that a QCC process that is rooted in the five core elements outlined in this chapter outperforms alternatives whether you are a doctor, CEO, first-time manager, or parent.

Ironically, the actions you intend to push on an employee are often similar to the activities reached from the pull approach. Similar solutions or activities are reached with two significant differences; mutual agreement by both parties, and a higher likelihood of execution. Accountability and ownership are transferred to the employee through the act of asking questions. This translates into improved follow-up and completion of the plan. People are simply more likely to take action on things that are not forced upon them or that they have concluded are the right action steps.

QCC is not possible if the employee is not interested in being coached. Both parties need skin in the game; each needs to be personally invested in the process. Coaching must be viewed as a partnership where everyone wins and it is not looked upon as a mandatory activity.

We acknowledge that not everyone wants to be coached. We get it, but that doesn't imply that we condone employees exempting themselves from the process. Last time we checked, managers are in charge. If a person doesn't want to work on Fridays, that doesn't mean the manager folds in to that request. The same holds true for coaching.

It is not your responsibility to "chase" a person or "persuade" him that coaching is worth his time. People need to understand the impact their choices have on their employment, especially in today's economic climate.

When mavericks are allowed to operate outside established rules, unrest increases among the team. A rogue individual may generate substantial results for the organization, but there are costs associated with their actions. These individuals hold you hostage by threatening to leave if they are not left alone. But their actions create a cancerous effect on overall morale and production of the greater team.

Former all-time home run leader Barry Bonds is an individual who was allowed to operate from a different set of rules than his San Francisco Giant teammates. He had his own section of the locker room, including his own recliner and big screen TV, and spent little time interacting with his teammates. His production on the field was significant, but his antics off the field were a constant distraction for the team, ultimately suppressing their overall success. In the end, the Giants chose not to keep Barry on the team after his value of filling seats during the home run chase had been fully utilized. Even the best hitter in baseball became expendable.

Employment (and, yes, this also includes agents, contractors and associates) involves operating within established ground rules associated with being on a team. Being employed is a two-way street. There are expectations that must be met in exchange for receiving a paycheck. One expectation is that people will be managed and coached. At the end of the day, managers are paid to generate results through their team. Coaching improves results. Therefore, employees cannot make themselves exempt from this important process. It is not their choice.

CLOSING THOUGHT

The five core elements of QCC are
(1) Consistent Process
(2) Predictable Frequency
(3) Coach to Relevant Topics
(4) Coach to Inputs and not Results
(5) Mutually Agreed-Upon Goals

Predictability when coaching drives behavioral changes. Conversations need to adhere to a repeatable process to maximize results. Repeatable doesn't mean that all individuals are coached exactly the same way, but it does mean there is consistency in coaching conversations. This consistency is what drives employee behavior changes. Coaching is an ongoing process and includes all members of a team. Although frequency and focus vary for each individual, good managers dedicate time to every member of their team.

Effective coaching is relevant to opportunities presented to the team and avoids generalities. Good coaches connect their efforts to activities that lead to performance improvement of their employees. Coaching is directed to real opportunities and must be done in a timely manner. Theoretical discussions don't advance development and have minimal impact on employee performance. Instead, discussions must be focused on key inputs that will drive improved results. Good coaches focus on changing process inputs to improve process results.

Lastly, strong coaches come to mutually agreed-to goals with the individuals they coach. They use questions to pull employees to a satisfactory conclusion without having to impose or push solutions on their employees.

CALL TO ACTION

- ❏ Proactively schedule a formal one-on-one coaching session with each member of your team. Start by scheduling a session with each person every other week. This will allow you to get in a groove and not over-commit, thereby requiring you to cancel a session.
- ❏ Use the Coaching Conversation Process as a guide to conduct your employee coaching sessions. Be sure to follow up on previous commitments prior to discussing new topics.
- ❏ Review the process you currently utilize to coach members of your team and evaluate deviations from the Coaching Conversation Process introduced in this chapter. For your next employee coaching session, select one step from the Coaching Conversation Process that you want to improve. Prior to the meeting, write down a brief plan of how you will execute this step, and complete a post-meeting self-assessment as to how you performed and what the impact was to the conversation.
- ❏ Focus on asking questions to pull mutually agreed-upon goals to the surface, rather than pushing your agenda. Prepare a list of questions prior to your coaching session to minimize the likelihood that you revert to making statements.

SECTION 2

The Fundamentals of Questions

Chapter 6
The Importance of Trust

In Section I, we introduced the fundamentals of coaching. We outlined the importance for managers to be predictable in the frequency in which they coach their teams and how their conversations are structured. We examined the need for managers to make coaching conversations relevant by discussing specific situations rather than being generic and theoretical. We emphasized the importance of developing mutually agreed-upon goals by asking instead of telling, pulling versus pushing.

This is not a book about coaching theory, simply providing you with thought-provoking concepts. The goal of this book is to challenge traditional thinking and provide a means to immediately apply new knowledge into your management practices.

Developing mutually agreed-upon goals by pulling versus pushing sounds pretty theoretical. Conceptually, the pull versus push analogy does a good job of providing a visual image that supports the strategy, but it lacks tactical details that allow execution. This analogy needs something to make it actionable. That something is questions. Level 3 Coaches understand the power of questions and how important they are in developing others. They understand the purpose of questions and are skilled at deploying them at the right time and in the right manner. Level 3 Coaches understand that questions:

- Shift the conversation to focus on the individual being coached
- Demonstrate interest and caring
- Allow for an accurate assessment of skills and capabilities
- Lead to a better understanding and agreement
- Channel the discussion to key activities
- Improve the participation level from the other party
- Provide a forum for the employee to voice concerns

The aforementioned list of benefits is quite compelling in terms of why you would choose to utilize QCC with your team. Becoming proficient with QCC appears to be straightforward, and in many ways it is. So you may think you're ready to start firing out questions in your next coaching session. However, the application of how to ask effective questions is more challenging than simply understanding the benefits. Just because we know something is the right thing to do doesn't mean we understand how to do it, or the intricacies of how to do it well.

To clarify this point, we reference an example many can relate to: the golf swing. Most amateur golfers understand the benefits of a good stance, the correct grip, and proper alignment to the ball. These three elements are discussed and demonstrated by golf professionals around the world. Why? Because the benefits are so significant.

The number of things that can go wrong the moment the club head moves away from the ball on the backswing are too numerous to count and can be overwhelming to think about. Most amateurs understand that their opportunity to hit a good shot gets exponentially smaller if the proper stance, grip, and alignment aren't in place before the club head ever moves. If the setup isn't correct, the typical golfer is already at a significant disadvantage without even moving a muscle.

However, when a golfer establishes a good stance, utilizes a correct grip and has the proper alignment, good things happen. The ball will travel straighter. The ball will travel a greater distance along the right path, and the probability of a good shot is dramatically increased. These are clearly things we work hard to achieve on a golf course!

In regard to our respective golf games, the benefits of stance, grip, and proper alignment are not in question. We get it. However, just as with questions in coaching, simply understanding the benefits doesn't automatically translate into effective execution of the process. If it did, our golf games would be much better than they currently are, and golf pros wouldn't still be coaching these same fundamentals. Lucky for them, the application of this knowledge is much more difficult than obtaining the knowledge itself.

Just as there are fundamentals in golf, QCC has its own fundamentals listed on the following page:

KEY CONCEPT

The Essentials of QCC

1. *The Importance of Trust*
2. *Question Basics*
3. *The Strategic Use of Questions*

The Importance of Trust

Trust is a key ingredient for successful relationships. This is true personally and professionally. How many marriages break up due to a lack of trust? How many friendships are strained? How many employees don't trust that their manager has their best interests at heart? Short answer, way too many! It is difficult to maintain a healthy relationship when you are constantly wondering if the other party cares about your success. Eventually, this consumes your thoughts and takes a significant physical and emotional toll, often resulting in irreconcilable differences.

How does trust relate to asking questions? To illustrate the connection, we use the example of being in a relationship that lacks trust. How would you react if your significant other asked the following questions when you walked in the door after a late night at the office? "Where have you been?" "What have you been doing?" "Why are you home so late?"

You might feel defensive, frustrated, or even angry. You may feel insulted to be interrogated when you were simply working late to meet a critical deadline for your boss. The questions add tension to the relationship. Emotions run high. Voices are raised. All from three simple questions! However, upon further digging it becomes clear questions are not the root of these feelings. The underlying problem is the lack of trust between you and your significant other. Questions simply expose and irritate this lack of trust. In a healthy relationship with abundant trust, those same questions lead the conversation down a different path.

A Personal Experience – A Loss of Trust

Early in my career, I was recruited by the leader of a progressive organization to join their senior leadership team. It was an exciting opportunity. I greatly enjoyed and respected this individual as a leader. The business had an outstanding reputation locally and nationally. The team I would be leading was very talented. The job was a great fit from every perspective. Everything was perfect.

The first several years in the job were some of the most enjoyable of my career. I was highly engaged. I was closely connected to the leader that hired me. We communicated frequently and openly. We had lunch together several times a week and talked openly about the challenges and opportunities ahead. The future was bright and it was invigorating to operate in such a high trust environment. We achieved phenomenal organizational success.

Then something changed. It is hard to pinpoint the exact time or event that triggered the change, but there was no denying things were different. Lunch invitations stopped coming, the frequency of conversations dwindled, and when they did, they had a different tone and focused on narrower less interesting topics. Trust was lost.

Questions asked now took on a different tone. They seemed to be targeted at exposing shortcomings instead of generating dialogue and development. I found myself over thinking my responses as to avoid being tripped up and potentially saying something wrong.

This had a negative effect on my engagement and performance. Work was not nearly as rewarding as it used to be. Rather than being invigorated and energized, I was drained. I spent time worrying about what caused this situation instead of focusing on the task at hand. It became more and more consuming and began leaking into my personal life. It was not the type of situation that drove peak performance. It was one of the low points in an otherwise invigorating career. It all revolved around the deterioration of trust between manager and employee.

QCC is a powerful means to develop others. Asking questions is more effective than making statements and telling employees what to do. However, as with any management practice performed poorly, coaching with questions can have negative consequences if not used with positive intent.

It's all about trust. The level of trust between two people has a significant impact on the underlying tone and intent of questions. The stronger the trust, the more positive people respond to questions. This realization led us to develop a simple but powerful model called the Question Continuum©.

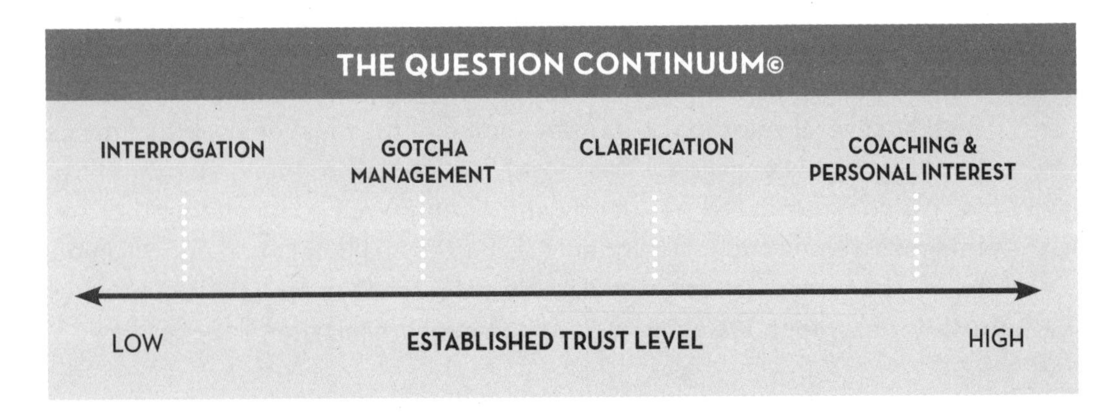

The Question Continuum underscores different scenarios in which questions are asked, and the result of their use in those situations. In addition, it provides the foundation for an enormously important component of asking questions: the establishment of trust between the manager and employee.

The Question Continuum illustrates an important point. You can ask the exact same question to two different people, yet it can be perceived differently based on the level of trust established between the two individuals. To illustrate, let's walk through the Continuum from left to right.

Interrogation

The left end of the Question Continuum represents interrogation. Asking questions of someone with whom there is absolutely no trust. Someone knows something that the other person wants, and that person will go to extreme lengths to obtain that information. Questions are asked over again and again until the victim capitulates. We have all seen TV dramas or big-screen movies depicting this horrible process. A person tied to a chair in a dark, damp room, with a bright light shining in their eyes. The interrogators use a variety of psychological ploys to break the person being questioned: multiple interrogators, good guys, bad guys, one-on-one, or triple-teamed. You get the picture!

Not exactly a pleasant experience or one that conjures up warm and fuzzy feelings about the use of questions. What poor soul wants to be put through the rigor of defensively answering 20 questions prior to going into an important meeting? When questions are used in an interrogative manner, it automatically puts a person on the defensive and makes him question his answers and behaviors. This erodes confidence and stifles growth.

For many managers, QCC is a completely new style and approach. The more traditional and direct the existing management style, the more pronounced the change. This change will not go unnoticed by the team. The shift to asking questions when coaching needs to be preceded by establishing trust with those individuals. Without trust, their perception of QCC may favor the left end of the Question Continuum.

So the comparison of interrogation to coaching is a little absurd. It is ridiculous to visualize an employee tied to a chair answering questions from her manager with a bright light shining in her eyes. (Unless, of course, it is the end of the year and they are way behind on their goals!)

However, it is not too far-fetched to have an individual feel as though he is being interrogated by his manager, constantly having to respond to a barrage of never-ending questions with an accusatory overtone. Employee performance will decline if this continues over time. Another personal experience illustrates this point well.

A Personal Experience – The Rookie and the Veterans

As a young salesperson, I had the opportunity to make a joint sales call with a seasoned veteran from my company. This would be a stressful situation for many, but it was magnified in this case because I was charged with leading the call. Oh, and by the way, this was also the very first call of my career!

Unfortunately, it started poorly and went downhill from there. Immediately out of customer earshot, the veteran began firing sharp, closed-ended questions at me. The point of the questions was not to offer suggestions; on the contrary, the questions were used to emphasize mistakes. The intent of my manager was to show me how incompetent I was. The manager had little desire to develop my skills.

Fortunately, everyone deserves another chance. With a slightly bruised ego, I got my opportunity on my very next call, this time with a different veteran sales manager. The call was only slightly more successful, but the post-call discussion was what stuck in my mind. In this case, the manager asked me a series of insightful open-ended questions. These questions were not used to exploit weaknesses. Their intent was to challenge my thinking and strategies used in the call, and explore ways in which to leverage this knowledge in the future.

It is apparent that the tone of an interrogative session is very different than the tone of a coaching session, even when asking the very same questions. The tone in one scenario is laced with accusation, and the tone in the other is charged with support.

A large part of what drives perception is intent. Are the questions being asked to catch someone in a lie, or are the questions being utilized to help her get better? The source of what drives the difference in perception is trust.

When a manager establishes trust with their team, questions take on a very different tone. They are not perceived as threatening; instead they sound positive and introspective. They positively challenge the other person and help develop her thinking. Let's demonstrate.

Think about how you would feel being asked the following questions from a manager with whom you had a poor relationship that lacked trust. The type of relationship where you were constantly on pins and needles, wondering if your manager thought you were spending time on the right activities.

1. What do you have going on next week?
2. Why are you meeting with Shari?
3. What value do you see in working on this project?

When these questions are asked under the pretense of having little established trust, you might respond defensively and feel threatened or frustrated. These questions imply you don't know what you are doing, you lack good judgment, and you require micro-managing from your boss. They don't create a sense of empowerment. They sap your energy and motivation, and if repeated on a consistent basis, could potentially drive you from the organization. All this from a brief exchange of questions that were asked without established trust between two individuals!

Gotcha Management

Let's shift our attention to the next delineation on the Question Continuum; Gotcha Management.

Gotcha Management exists when there is a lack of trust between the coach and employee — so little trust that the manager is using questions to trip up the individual and catch him doing or saying something incorrect. It is impossible to confuse Gotcha Management with positive intent because with Gotcha Management the primary motive is to punish the employee or prove the superiority of the manager.

A scenario involving Gotcha Management could have the manager exposing an employee who has ignored a required activity. Rather than addressing this in a constructive manner, and going into the conversation with positive intent, the manager asks questions to implicate the subordinate. Upon implication, the manager takes punitive action.

Let's illustrate Gotcha Management with an example near and dear to many employees — timely completion and submission of expense reports. In this scenario, the manager (MGR) is well aware the expense reports in question have not been turned in on time, yet he still asks the question to catch and punish the employee (EE).

MGR: Trey, didn't we agree that monthly expense reports were to be turned in within one week after month end?

EE: Yes we did.

MGR: Well, did you get yours in on time? (Already knowing the answer)

EE: No, I didn't.

MGR: Fine; you make this hard on me, I'll make it hard on you. I'm going to delay approving your expenses until you get this right.

The mindset for the manager entering that conversation was to root out and exterminate this poor behavior. Guilt was assumed going in, correctly or incorrectly, and the interaction had minimal likelihood to end positively. Lack of trust was a significant factor in this discussion.

Clarification

Let's review this same scenario assuming a solid level of established trust between the manager and employee. We are moving right on the Question Continuum to Clarification.

In this case, the manager has the same evidence exposing the employee not performing a required activity. Rather than taking a punitive approach, the manager enters this discussion with positive intent. Because trust exists, this positive intent is transparent to the employee, both in action and tone. The same questions are asked, but their purpose is to clarify understanding of the situation. Punishment is not the pre-determined outcome of this process.

MGR: Trey, I need to visit with you about your expenses. Do you recall our conversation on timely submission of expense reports?

EE: Yes, I think so, why?

MGR: Well, did you get yours in on time?

EE: No, at least not on time, but it's really no big deal anyway. You pay me to manage our offices and not fill out paperwork, right?

MGR: I certainly pay you to manage our offices, but let's talk about why this is a big deal. On average, what would you estimate your expenses to be?

EE: Roughly between $2500 and $3500 per month.

MGR: That sounds about right, as I believe your travel and expense budget is around $40K a year. Now multiply that by your 6 counterparts across the region, and you start to get some pretty big numbers.

EE: I suppose so. I didn't think of it that way. Wow, annually that is almost two-hundred and fifty thousand dollars, isn't it?

MGR: Yep, so how do you think it impacts things when you are late with your report?

EE: To tell you the truth, I have no idea. I guess it could make it difficult for us to manage the budget and have an accurate picture from a cash flow perspective. I know I don't like it when I get a late bill from a company regarding my home expenses. It kind of throws a wrench in the system.

MGR: **Exactly. Expense report reimbursements are a big deal for us. Timely submission of expenses helps the company with predictable cash flow and helps keep our costs lower. If we keep our costs lower, how does that ultimately affect you?**

EE: *I would like to think that if the company has lower costs it would lower prices, which would be a big deal. Lower-priced products are a lot easier to sell.*

MGR: **Exactly, and yes, that is exactly our goal as a company. All that from you getting your expense reports in on time! There is one more thing that is important about this process. Our accounting team has goals around turn time and when expenses come in all bunched together instead of in a predictable flow, it negatively impacts their performance. This makes them grumpy, and I certainly don't like to work with grumpy accountants.**

EE: *Ok, I get it. I'll get them in on time.*

The mindset entering the conversation was clarification, followed by coaching the person to complete the agreed-upon activities. Additional questions may be used to understand why the process is not being performed, and how this can be improved. True understanding of the cause is important to the manager. This understanding translates effectively into subsequent coaching.

Coaching and Personal Interest

Coaching and Personal Interest is depicted on the far right end of the Question Continuum, and represents a high trust relationship between manager and employee. A mutual understanding exists that the manager is genuinely interested in the development of the employee. There is not an undertone of fear on behalf of the employee when she is asked questions by her manager.

Previously, we asked how you would feel being asked questions from a manager with whom you had a poor relationship that lacked trust. This created the perception of being interrogated. This time, consider how you would feel being asked those same questions, but by a manager with whom you had an excellent relationship; a relationship where trust was not an issue and you knew the manager was committed to your success.

1. What do you have going on next week?
2. Why are you meeting with Shari?
3. What value do you see in working on this project?

Your reaction this time is different. Although they are the same questions, you feel constructively challenged and supported. You are not threatened because you know your manager has a vested interest in your success. You recognize these questions are being asked to ensure you are investing time in areas that will pay the biggest dividends. If you succeed, your manager succeeds. Very different reactions when compared to the previous scenario. This illustrates the importance of establishing high-trust relationships and operating on the right end of the Question Continuum. It is the gateway to high performance coaching and increased leverage.

CLOSING THOUGHT

QCC can only be successful if built upon a foundation of trust. Without trust, employees will be reluctant to answer questions honestly and progress from coaching will be limited.

The Question Continuum illustrates an important point. You can ask exactly the same question to two different people, yet it can be perceived differently based on the level of trust established between the two individuals. The Question Continuum© is delineated into four levels; (1) Interrogation (2) Gotcha Management (3) Clarification and (4) Coaching and Personal Interest.

CALL TO ACTION

- ❑ **How often do you ask employees questions to which you already know the answer? Is your objective in doing so to punish the individual, or help them learn?**
- ❑ **Evaluate the level of established trust you have with each member of your team. Mark the specific level using the Question Continuum diagram.**
- ❑ **Identify specific action that can be taken to improve the level of trust to the next delineation to the right on the Question Continuum.**

Chapter 7
Question Basics

In Chapter 6, we introduced the essentials of QCC and explored the importance of trust and introducing the Question Continuum. We now shift our attention to the second essential element of QCC, which is having knowledge about the basics of questions.

KEY CONCEPT

The Essentials of QCC

1. *The Importance of Trust*
2. *Question Basics*
3. *The Strategic Use of Questions*

Question Basics

Your ability to ask effective questions is essential in creating an environment with your team that is conducive to effective communication. Questions pave the way for two-way conversations, shift the attention away from you, and begin the process of establishing trust. If honest and open dialogue between you and your team member is not achieved, the likelihood of effective communication is greatly diminished.

As a manager, you must ask the right questions at the right time in order to gain a better understanding of the skills and knowledge of your team, a necessity of coaching. Level 1 Coaches are not equipped to effectively perform this task.

Asking questions is a learned skill. As with the development of any skill, a solid foundation of knowledge on which that skill is built increases the likelihood of mastery. While asking questions may be natural to some, it is a skill that needs to be studied, understood, and practiced by most. The skill of asking effective questions won't improve without practice, self-assessment, and more practice.

Asking random diagnostic questions to an employee does not automatically qualify as coaching. There is more to it than simply asking questions. A strategy is necessary to leverage different types of questions at different times. An astute Level 3 Coach understands the purpose of these question types.

Too often managers ask diagnostic questions that are not supported or channeled by any strategy or logic. Questions, often of the same type, are asked with no end goal in mind.

"Channel Surfing"

We've all annoyed friends or family members by channel surfing, quickly switching channels without spending time going deep on any particular program. As different channels fly across the screen, the odds of catching something compelling are minimal. As a result, very little captures your interest and you are quickly on to the next station. You never realize what you could have learned if you had only stayed put on one channel for just a few more minutes.

When you 'surf' with questions that are not connected through strategy, the resulting coaching conversation has minimal impact, and does very little to develop the confidence, competence, and skills of your employee. Just as a TV viewer misses important information by rushing through the channels, often times you miss clues and opportunities for performance improvement by jumping from question to question. Too often you don't go deep and ask additional questions in any one specific area.

Surf's Up – So what does it sound like when you go surfing? Below are examples of good diagnostic questions, but used in an ineffective manner. They skim the surface on a number of unrelated topics and don't lend themselves to a logical destination for the conversation.

- How are things going?
- Are you spending a lot of time traveling?
- What challenges are you facing with your team?
- Did you get your expense report turned in on time?
- What is going on with your big project?
- What are you doing next week?
- How much overtime has your team logged this month?
- How are your expenses in comparison to your budget?

Put yourself in the shoes of the individual on the receiving end of the above questions. Would this be a helpful conversation? Possibly, but the odds are slim. It is scattered and not purposeful. As the recipient you walk away confused as to what you should focus on.

To effectively execute QCC, it is important that you understand the fundamental aspects of questions. This allows you to maximize coaching opportunities and engage employees in meaningful dialogue. Sometimes you are fooled into thinking you have asked the right questions, only to be surprised with a different and unexpected outcome. The story below provides a humorous example of an individual being caught in this situation.

A Funny Story about Asking Questions

A man goes to his country club to play golf, and gets paired up with a threesome, one of which is an 80-year-old man. As they are walking toward the first tee, the 80-year-old player acknowledges that his eyesight is not what it used to be, and as a result he always plays with a spotter. The spotter's job is to watch the ball as it approaches the target, and to make sure that he tracks the exact location of where the ball comes to rest.

The weather on this day was not very nice, as a slight drizzle fell. Because of the poor weather, there were not many caddies around the pro-shop. On most days his spotters were teenage caddies who had excellent vision, but today the only option was a gentleman who appeared to be well into his late 80's.

Upon discovering the age of the spotter, the golfer was obviously concerned whether the old man would be able to see the ball any better than he could. Because of this concern, he asked the spotter how good his vision was and whether he had had a recent eye exam. The spotter responded with an emphatic yes, and additionally provided that a recent eye exam found him to have perfect 20/20 vision.

Satisfied the spotter had great vision, they proceed to the first hole. The golfer hits his first shot right down the middle of the fairway and together they have no difficulty locating the ball. The golfer then sends the spotter up near the first green so that he can watch his approach shot come in. He hits a nice shot towards the green, but isn't sure where it actually ends up. He is not concerned, as he has a spotter with excellent vision who is positioned in exactly the right spot. He confidently approaches the green and excitedly asked the spotter if he saw his ball. To which the spotter replies, "YOU BET!" The golfer immediately inquires as to where exactly the ball is, to which the spotter replies, "I DON'T REMEMBER!"

Closed- and Open-Ended Questions

Closed-ended questions in coaching have a more limited role. This should be of no surprise, as one of the primary objectives of QCC is to get the person being coached engaged in the conversation. Closed-ended questions certainly don't accomplish this, but they are very useful in gaining clarity around specific issues throughout a coaching session. Examples of closed-ended questions include:

- What time did you arrive for the meeting?
- Was the room set up appropriately?
- Who attended?
- What documents did you hand out to participants?
- Was there consensus in the group?
- Were any conclusions reached?
- Did people take away specific actions?
- When will you follow up with the participants?

Other words found at the beginning of closed-ended questions include "where," "are," "which," "is," or "has."

You use closed-ended questions to obtain one-phrase answers, or simple yes / no responses. Responding to these types of questions doesn't require a great deal of thought on behalf of your employee. You would utilize closed-ended questions when coaching for several reasons: to confirm understanding from the other party, to limit the range of responses, and to channel the conversation in a desired direction.

You use open-ended questions to engage others in conversation, uncover specific needs, identify additional coaching opportunities, and elaborate on the understanding and application of knowledge covered in a one-on-one session. Examples include:

- How did the meeting go?
- Is there something you could have done differently to have made it more effective?
- Why were the participants interested in your presentation?
- What is keeping them from moving forward?
- What can I do to assist you with the next steps?

Open ended questions are the cornerstone for effective QCC conversations and often begin with "What," "Why," and "How." Talk time in traditional manager/employee conversations is dominated by the manager. QCC shifts the talk time from you to the person you are coaching, but in a directed and purposeful manner.

Open- and closed-ended questions are used in combination at the beginning, middle, and end of a coaching session. We previously introduced the Coaching Conversation Process, shown below, to provide a consistent model to guide your conversations. We now overlay an inventory of open- and closed-ended questions to potentially use at each step of the process.

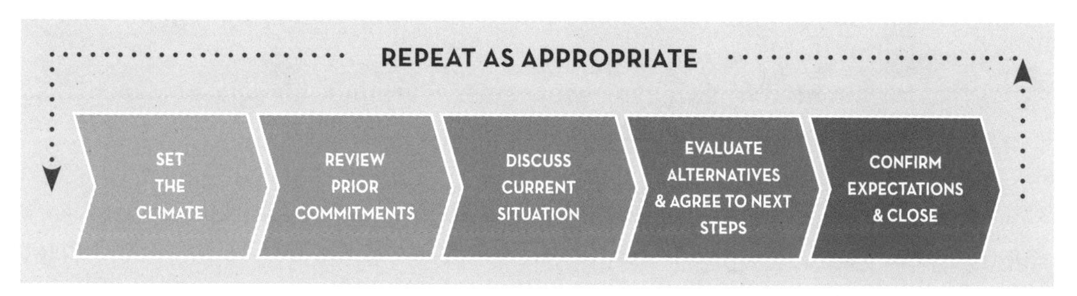

1. Set the climate (the questions to build rapport are examples only)

- How was your weekend? (Open)
- How did your (community, family, school) event go last week? (Open)
- Are you having a good week? (Closed)
- What is going on to make you feel that way? (Open)
- What topics did you have on your list to cover today? (Open)

2. Review Prior Commitments

- How have things been going since our last coaching conversation? (Open)
- Can you take a few minutes to recap the actions we agreed to in our last one-on-one? (Open)
- Do you feel good about your progress? Why? (Closed/Open)
- Which of the actions would you like to discuss first? (Closed)

3. Discuss Current Situation

- Related to the first action, what changes did you make following our last one-on-one conversation? (Open)
- What was the result of your making these changes?(Open)
- Did it achieve the desired results? (Closed)
- How do you know? What feedback did you receive from others? (Open)

4. Evaluate Alternatives and Agree to Next Steps

- How difficult will it be for you to continue this behavior? (Closed)
- What obstacles do you anticipate getting in the way? (Open)

- What ideas do you have to solidify this as a habit? (Open)
- Are their further opportunities for improvement? (Closed)
- What other ideas do you have to further improve in this area? (Open)

5. Confirm Expectations and Close

- Before we move to the next item, can you please provide a recap of what we agreed to? (Open)
- What do you need from me to ensure success around this action? (Open)
- When do you want to discuss this again? (Open)

The purpose of providing these questions is to jump-start your QCC process and improve your ability to navigate coaching conversations. Over time you will develop your own questions as you personalize the coaching process.

When setting the climate, it is important to build rapport with the individuals you coach. This involves asking questions about them and their areas of interest before diving into specific coaching topics. In the early stages of a coaching relationship, it is very important to establish expectations around how to maximize your time together. The questions provided under Step1 are examples only.

CLOSING THOUGHT

Effective managers recognize there is more to QCC than asking a random series of questions. When you "surf" with disjointed questions, you reduce the probability for employee learning, retention, and behavior changes. Level 2 and 3 Coaches understand the power of staying on one channel and concentrating questions to uncover opportunities and change behaviors.

Recognizing the differences and proper times to use open- and closed-ended questions will improve your effectiveness with QCC. Both question types are important, but they must be used in a planned and deliberate manner. They have different purposes and are interwoven into coaching conversations.

CALL TO ACTION

Following your next one-on-one coaching session with a member of your team, evaluate your effectiveness by answering the following questions:

- ❑ What percent of the meeting did you talk versus listen?
- ❑ Did you make more statements or ask more questions?
- ❑ When asking questions, were they open- or closed-ended? What impact did this have on the engagement level of the other person in the conversation?
- ❑ Did you reach resolution on the topics discussed?
- ❑ Did you follow the Coaching Conversation Process and the recommended questions? How can you make your next coaching conversation more effective?

Chapter 8
The Strategic Use of Questions

We previously introduced the core elements of QCC and explored the importance of trust and introducing *The Question Continuum*©. In Chapter 7, we explored the basics of questions, including different question types. We now shift our attention to the third essential of QCC, the Strategic Use of Questions.

Questions are an amazingly powerful tool in developing the thinking skills, knowledge, and confidence of others. We repeatedly witnessed individuals move from Level 1 to Level 2 Coaches as they became more proficient at asking questions. As they moved to this higher level, the engagement of their employees improved, as did the employees' measured performance. However, as outlined in the last chapter, it takes more to achieve these results than simply asking a random series of simple questions.

As described above, we knew what we saw. However, as we studied questions in more depth, it became apparent there was a science behind what we were experiencing. One particular body of research which reaffirmed our thinking was that of Dr. Benjamin S. Bloom, an American Educational Psychologist, who in 1956 developed a system of learning behavior categories officially known as Bloom's Taxonomy. (Bloom, Benjamin S. *Taxonomy of Educational Objectives: The Classification of Educational Goals.* Susan Fauer Company, Inc., 1956. Print.)

What Bloom articulated in his work was that 95% of the questions students encountered on tests required them to think on the lowest possible level, specifically involving recall and recognition of facts. Bloom believed that education should focus on the "mastery" of subjects through higher-order thinking. In other words, the goal is to help students improve their critical thinking skills, not simply transfer information and facts. Clearly, this is a much different form of personal development, and one that provides a more rewarding experience for the student. By asking questions that involve higher-order thinking skills, students were able to evaluate situations more critically and retain information more readily.

Bloom's work reaffirmed there is more to asking questions than meets the eye. Your goal when asking an employee questions must go beyond her simply regurgitating facts and figures, the lowest form of thinking. The objective is to equip her to think through future situations without your guidance. If not, leverage will never be created.

As we contemplated Bloom's work and compared it to what we saw when observing managers coach their employees, it reinforced the importance of establishing a road map for how to ask more strategic questions. Asking strategic questions is not the kind of skill that people can do without a deliberate methodology. In doing so, we created the four Strategic Question Categories denoted below:

KEY CONCEPT

Strategic Question Categories

1. Diagnostic

2. Satisfaction

3. Sizing

4. Resolution

Each of the four question categories has a strategic purpose. One is not more effective than another, and they are not intended to be used independently. The power lies in how the question categories are used in combination, each one building on the previous, as you work through a specific issue with members of your team. This is illustrated in the diagram below.

To better explain this concept, we refer back to our "surfing" analogy. Rapidly changing TV channels is a good strategy if the goal is to skim small bits of information on a broad range of topics. It is not a good strategy if the goal is to go deep on

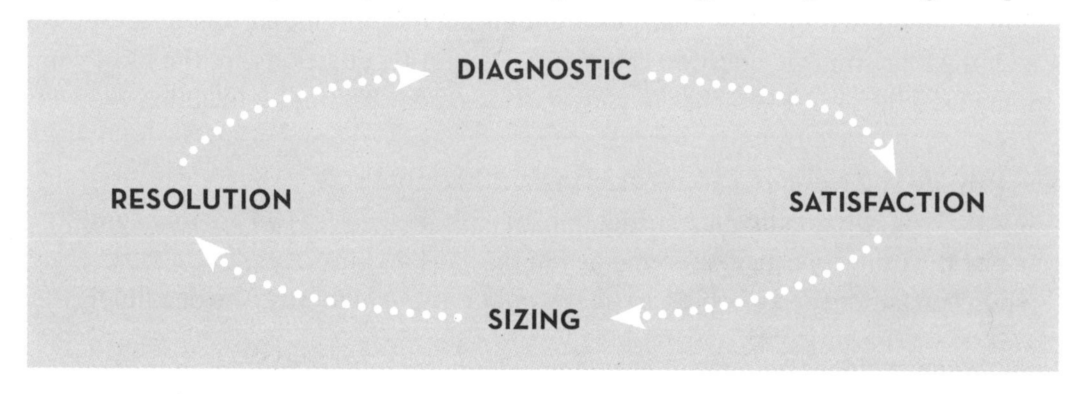

one specific topic. The same can be said with QCC. Asking a multitude of questions without an underlying strategy results in small bits of information gleaned over a broad range of topics. This is frustrating to the person on the receiving end of what appears to be random series of questions. In this case, more is less.

A common coaching mistake is to address too many issues simultaneously. You want instantaneous results, so you spread your coaching focus over an array of issues. Although you perceive that a lot of ground is being covered, the probability of modifying employee behavior and sustaining new habits over an extended period of time is minimal. People have limited capacity. QCC is most effective when you stay on a "single channel" in a coaching session and go deep into one or two topics — the opposite of surfing.

KEY CONCEPT

Focus questions on one or two key topics.

Over the remainder of this chapter we explore each of the four question categories in detail. Following are definitions for each category, plus examples in the context of the employee being a project manager.

1. Diagnostic questions are used to collect background information and ***assess*** the skills, knowledge, and effectiveness of the employee you are coaching. The purpose of Diagnostic questions is to fact find and discover performance improvement opportunities for your team member.

Diagnostic questions are often closed-ended. That does not imply they always seek a yes or no response; rather, they can be used to elicit a very specific and defined response.

Of the four strategic question categories, Diagnostic questions are the most commonly used by Level 1 Coaches in conversations today. Examples include:

- How do you feel about your performance this month?
- Are things progressing according to plan with the project you are managing?
- Are the project participants engaged in the work?
- Do you anticipate any obstacles that would cause you to miss the deadline?

2. Satisfaction questions follow Diagnostic questions. You ask Satisfaction questions to determine whether your employee is content with his performance in a particular area. Satisfaction questions start the improvement process by creating a sense of urgency on behalf of the person being coached. The purpose of Satisfaction questions is to move beyond fact-finding, and create the desire to take action and improve performance. Coaching is a ***mutually*** agreed-upon process between you and the employee. Mutual doesn't mean the other individual is along for the ride doing whatever you tell them to do. They are a partner in the process.

Examples of Satisfaction questions are:

- Are you satisfied with the overall progress of the project you are managing?
- How is the work balanced between the different project participants? Are you satisfied with everyone's level of involvement?
- Is the rate at which people are working outside the meetings satisfactory?

3. Sizing questions follow Satisfaction questions, and are asked to help the employee understand the ***cost*** or ***significance*** of the issue being discussed. The objective of Sizing questions is to ***quantify*** a problem, or opportunity, for the person being coached so they are compelled to take action. The power of Sizing questions is that they create a sense of urgency for the employee, but do so without making statements, leading to much greater buy-in and sustainability of action.

Examples of Sizing questions might sound something like this:

- If the team is unable to deliver the project on time, what impact will that have on the business by not having the new training available?
- If you don't hit all the project milestones, how will that affect your bonus?
- If you could increase the time the participants work outside the project team by 15%, how would that affect the team's ability to get things wrapped up?

4. Resolution questions follow Sizing questions, and are asked to gain a commitment from the person being coached and initiate a call to action. ***The objective of Resolution questions is to reach agreement and develop a mutually agreed-upon plan*** to address the identified performance issues.

Examples of Resolution questions are:

- Are you interested in us developing a plan together to elevate your performance in these areas?

- Would you like my help?
- Would you like to spend some time together creating strategies on how you can achieve this?

A properly asked Resolution question at the conclusion of the process stimulates the other person to take action.

Let's walk through a conversation where a sales manager (SM) utilizes questions from each category, going deep to drive impact with the employee (EE).

SM: **So Mitch, how do you feel about your performance this month? (Diagnostic)**

EE: Not bad. Certainly not where I want to be, but considering some of the challenges in my market I am pleased with my performance.

SM: **Do you think you have enough leads to keep the front end of your pipeline full? (Diagnostic)**

EE: Yes. There always seem to be enough quality prospects in my territory.

SM: **Of the leads that you work, how is your pull through rate? (Diagnostic)**

EE: My pull through rate is very low in comparison to other people on the team. Year to date, I am signing approximately 8% of the prospects worked. Last time I checked, the team and industry average were sitting at around 15%. I know Mason closes approximately 22% of his opportunities and leads the team.

SM: **So is this something you are interesting in improving? (Satisfaction)**

EE: Absolutely. As I think about it, this is limiting my performance.

SM: **How many deals are you losing per month due to your low close rate in comparison to the team average? (Sizing)**

EE: Good question. Let me think.... I target about 20 new leads per month. Projecting forward, an 8% close rate on 20 prospects is 1.6 deals. If I could improve my close rate to the team average of 15%, that would be 3 deals per month, or an additional 1.5 deals!

SM: **How big is your average deal? What impact would this have on your goals? (Sizing)**

EE: My average sale is $100K, so getting an additional 1.5 deals per month would equate to $150K of new business.... that totals over a million dollars a year. Wow, that would go along ways towards my $1.2M annual new business goal!

SM: **Are you interested in spending some time together to talk about how we might increase your close rate from where it is today? (Resolution)**

EE: Absolutely. That sounds like a really good place to focus my time and attention.

Think about the end result of this conversation. Was Mitch forced to work in an area that he didn't see the importance of working? Was he a passenger in the conversation, or an active participant? Does Mitch have ownership to develop the solution, or is the manager going to have to police him to improve in this area?

Only time will tell. However, the manager did an excellent job of asking questions from the four strategic question categories; Diagnostic, Satisfaction, Sizing, and Resolution. This kept the discussion from wandering and losing effectiveness. The end result is a mutually agreed upon focus on a constrained part of the sales process. Mitch is vested in developing his skills in this area because the manager asked questions that framed up the significance of doing so.

Sure, this is a scripted role-play, and it is not realistic that every conversation will flow this well. However, think about how much more effective your conversations could be if you made incremental improvements, or made sure to include a Sizing question in your coaching conversations? Executing a conversation of this quality takes forethought and practice. It is a learned skill.

Because the use of strategic questions in a coaching conversation is so important, below is a second example which involves a different scenario. This conversation takes place between an operations director (OD) that oversees multiple doctors' offices and one of their office managers (OM).

OD: So how do you feel about the performance of your office this month? (Diagnostic)

OM: Things are going pretty well. We have our new receptionists fully trained and that has really helped patient flow.

OD: Has that helped decrease the patient wait time that your office was previously experiencing? (Diagnostic)

OM: Yes. Our wait time in the lobby is at an acceptable level.

OD: What has the impact been to patient satisfaction scores? (Diagnostic)

OM: That is an interesting question. I really thought that with our new receptionist in place our patient satisfaction scores would improve, but we are still running well below our targets.

OD: Have you looked into what might be causing this? (Diagnostic)

OM: Yes. It appears that patients have to wait a long time in the exam rooms once they are checked in and we take their vitals. This surprised me, but I guess most of my focus lately has been up front with our new receptionist. The average wait time in the exam rooms is almost 25 minutes.

OD: So is that wait time in the exam room satisfactory? (Satisfaction)

OM: No, not at all. When I first took this job we typically had wait times of less than 12 minutes. 25 minutes is very unacceptable.

OD: How much impact do you think the exam room wait time has on patient satisfaction scores? (Sizing)

OM: *Good question. It is significant. I know this because just last week I had two patients complain to me about the wait time and they scored us very low on their satisfaction scores. Based on information from my peers, they say every 10-minute reduction in wait time increases satisfaction scores by a full point.*

OD: Would you like to spend some time talking about how we can reduce the exam room wait time, ultimately improving your customer satisfaction scores? (Resolution)

OM: *That would be very helpful, yes.*

QCC is a potent strategy to develop individuals on your team while simultaneously improving your position of leverage as a manager. The foundation of QCC is built on your ability to harness the power of questions; the various types, their intent, and the means in which they are used. As with Bloom's Taxonomy, the objective of the four Strategic question types is to develop the higher order thinking skills of the person being coached. This requires knowledge, understanding, preparation, and practice.

CLOSING THOUGHT

This chapter introduced the Strategic Question Categories. These question categories are interdependent and used in combination when working through a QCC conversation. The objective of this framework is to develop the higher level thinking skills of the individuals with whom you coach. One reason coaching conversations often don't produce the desired results is because you try to cover too many topics in one sitting. You skim the surface over a broad range of issues, not making meaningful progress in any one area. By using the Strategic Question Categories, you are able to go deep in one area and gain buy-in and action from your team member. The Strategic Question Categories are (1) Diagnostic, (2) Satisfaction, (3) Sizing, and (4) Resolution.

Diagnostic questions are used in coaching to collect background information and assess the skills, knowledge, and effectiveness of your team member. Diagnostic questions are used to fact-find, validate, and identify coaching opportunities.

Satisfaction questions follow Diagnostic questions. You ask these questions to determine whether your team member is content with her performance in a particular area.

Sizing questions follow Satisfaction questions. You ask these questions to help the employee understand the cost or significance of the issue at hand. The objective of Sizing questions is to quantify a problem for the employee in such a manner that he is compelled to take action.

Resolution questions follow Sizing questions and are asked to gain a commitment from your team member and initiate a call to action. The objective of Resolution questions is to reach agreement and develop a mutually agreed-upon plan to address the identified opportunities.

CALL TO ACTION

Following your next one-on-one coaching session with a member of your team, evaluate your effectiveness by answering the following questions:

- ❑ Did you "change channels" and "surf" over multiple topics, or did you stay on the one channel and go deep into the topic at hand?
- ❑ Write down the questions you asked, and label each one with the appropriate category; Diagnostic, Satisfaction, Sizing, and Resolution. Did you ask questions from each of the four categories? If not, how would the conversation have been different had you included questions from the missing category?
- ❑ Take 30 minutes prior to your next coaching conversation and write down questions from each of the four question categories. Be sure the questions are specific to the individual needs of that team member. Make a concentrated effort to ask questions from each category. At the conclusion of the meeting, evaluate how well you did at utilizing questions and what adjustments need to be made to improve your next conversation.

SECTION 3

Implementing the Fundamentals

Chapter 9

Identifying Where to Coach

Section one detailed the differences between coaching and managing and introduced the core elements of QCC: utilizing the Coaching Conversation Process, establishing a predictable frequency to meet with your employees, and making coaching relevant by focusing on real situations effecting your team, and developing mutually agreed-upon goals.

We emphasized the importance of ***proactively coaching inputs*** versus ***reactively managing results***. Telling someone to improve their performance by 10% without helping them understand *how*, is not coaching. Level 3 Coaches coach to process inputs that correlate to process outputs.

The mechanical components of QCC are important and provide a foundation from which to build a coaching culture. However, the foundation is not complete without another key building block — understanding ***how*** to apply and execute a QCC strategy. This chapter explores the first of three core elements of how to execute QCC.

KEY CONCEPT

Core Elements of How to Execute QCC

1. *Identifying Where to Coach*
2. *Coaching to Strengths*
3. *Being Prepared*

1. ***Identifying Where to Coach*** – Managing a team of people presents a myriad of challenges. Things move at a rapid pace and pressure for improved results is ever-increasing. You are simultaneously pulled in different directions and forced to react to issues requiring immediate attention. E-mails pile up in your inbox. People constantly come to you with questions and approval requests. You hop from conference

call to conference call with no breaks. Before you know it, the week is over and it is difficult to recall what you accomplished. It is difficult to execute a proactive QCC approach when operating in an environment that breeds urgency.

In addition to operating in an urgent environment, you may ***lack clarity in terms of where to focus your coaching.*** This isn't because there aren't enough coaching opportunities available. In fact, the opposite is true in that there are more coaching opportunities than hours in the day. Without a disciplined and targeted approach, you will find yourself bouncing from issue to issue like a pinball, diluting your efforts and impact.

How and where you direct your coaching efforts is no different than managing any constrained resource. ***Level 3 Coaches evaluate the impact of their efforts and understand the payback for each hour invested with employees.***

Are you deliberate in how you invest your time, or is it more of an afterthought? Do you look back at the end of the week only to realize that little was accomplished? Level 3 Coaches evaluate their effectiveness and recalibrate their plan to avoid going into the next week using the same flawed approach. If you don't take this approach, your coaching focus is reactive and haphazard. This creates a vicious cycle as you are too busy to take a step back and evaluate whether you are working on the right issues. You go into coaching conversations unprepared and don't spend time in areas that yield the greatest return on time.

QCC is a continuous process. Coaching employees is ongoing, including time spent with top performers. This continuous nature requires an effective strategy to target coaching efforts. Without good targeting, significant time is wasted.

A valuable targeting approach used to identify where to invest coaching efforts involves the use of a pipeline tool. Organizations use pipeline data to quantify the volume of work flowing through key processes. Doctors' offices monitor patient flow, manufacturers evaluate orders flowing through the factory, retailers track inventory turns, service centers track call volume and talk time, and sales organizations quantify the number and size of deals at different stages in the sales cycle. Complex spreadsheets calculate pull-through rates for each section of the pipeline and often project cash flow and profitability. Pipeline or forecasting reports are fundamental to effectively running an organization.

For many of you, this is nothing new. We understand that. Why then are we including it in this book? The reason is simple. The pipeline is an important tool for you to diagnose ***where*** to coach.

Many of you use pipeline reports as a ***management*** tool. You monitor work flow and identify when things get bogged down. You send e-mails to employees to get updates as to when the problem will be resolved and the item will move to the next stage in the pipeline. These are important ***management*** activities, but it is equally important to use the pipeline as a ***coaching*** tool.

To illustrate this concept, consider an example that everyone can personally relate to: going to a doctor's office for an annual physical. Let's review the process at a high level and consider the major activities associated with this type of visit:

- Arrive at the office and check in with the receptionist
- Provide your insurance card and other personal information
- Sit in the waiting area until summoned by the nurse
- Go to the back area with the nurse, who records your weight, escorts you to an exam room, and takes your vitals
- Sit in the exam room until the doctor arrives
- Answer questions from the doctor and receive a complete physical exam
- Sit in the exam room until a person from the lab comes to draw your blood
- Original nurse comes back to exam room with your paperwork
- Proceed to checkout and provide payment for services

There are many places in this pipeline where patient flow can become "clogged." You could experience delays in the waiting room after having checked in with the receptionist. You might find yourself in another "clog" as you sit in the exam room unattended. You may experience yet another "clog" as you have to wait for someone from the lab to draw your blood. Finally, you could experience more delays at checkout if there are problems with your insurance or paperwork.

This example is not intended to condemn the health care system. In fact, many visits to the doctor are seamless and you experience no such delays. Our point of using a doctor's office visit is to simply illustrate a process that is easy to visualize.

Now let's tie this example back to coaching by looking at this process from the lens of the office manager. The manager is interested in eliminating patient delays for several reasons. They want patients to have good experiences so they will come back for more visits versus selecting a different doctor. Also, the more optimal the patient flow, and the more patients seen on a daily or weekly basis, the more revenue the office generates. Clogged patient pipelines are not good for business any way you look at it. The manager needs to understand where to focus her attention to improve the overall performance of the office. Where does the manager coach her teams, and what types of questions should she ask?

So if you are the office manager, how do you use the context of this pipeline scenario to diagnose where to coach and work "on" the system?

For starters, it requires evaluating where the patient pipeline gets clogged most frequently; do patients get stacked up at check-in, in the waiting room, in the exam room, at the lab, or at checkout? You must elevate your vantage point and view the system holistically.

Consider the implications if you don't identify the bottleneck correctly. For this example we designate the lab as the main bottleneck, or source of patient delays, for the office. There are no measurable patient flow delays before or after the lab. Therefore, if the office manager misdiagnoses the source of the problem and focuses her effort in another part of the system, it will have no measurable impact on patient flow and could actually make the problem worse.

For example, think through the ramifications if the manager incorrectly assumes the problem is at patient check-in. The staff makes changes to this part of the process and patients are now checked in to the office faster. However, patient flow still clogs up in the exam room when patients wait for lab personnel. The problem is actually worse because now there are even more patients stuck in the exam rooms when compared to before the process change.

This is a simple example of how good intentions often go awry. It also underscores the importance of using the pipeline concept to diagnose where to focus your coaching efforts.

Now consider another example to illustrate this point, this time going into more detail about how you can use data and measurement to diagnose where to coach your employees. Below is the pipeline referenced previously, which represents a typical sales process in a financial services organization.

This particular pipeline monitors sales performance for the business. The associated reports identify how many prospects are targeted, how many prospects are actively engaged with the sales team, and how many deals are projected to close by a specific date. Very important information if you are the sales manager.

So how do you tap into the potential of this tool and use it to ***diagnose*** and ***target*** coaching opportunities? It requires breaking several pipeline paradigms.

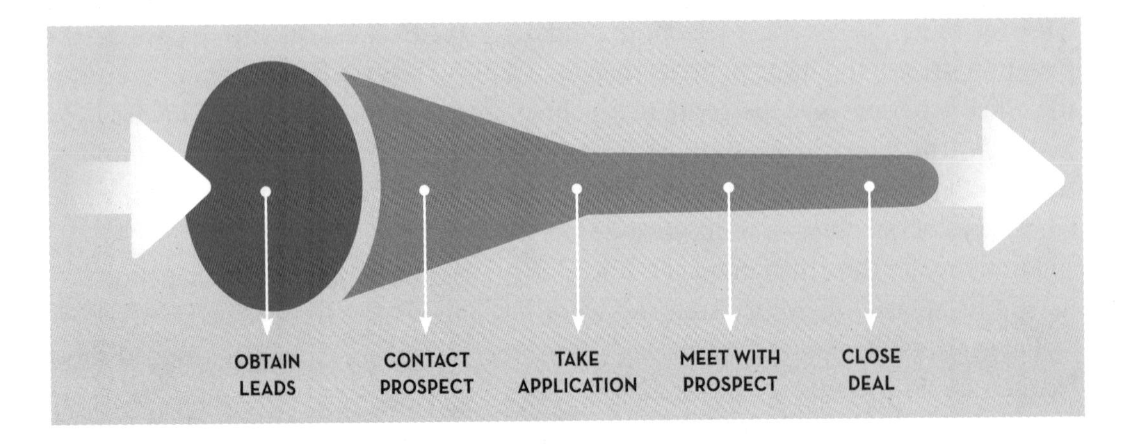

Pipeline Paradigm #1 – Coach to Individuals and Not Averages

The first paradigm involves how managers traditionally view pipeline performance. Level 1 Coaches manage to the ***average*** pull-through rate for each stage of the pipeline above. These averages are comprised of the individual performance results for each person on the team. When the average in one section is disproportionately low, Level 1 Coaches focus their efforts with everyone in that particular area. The logic used assumes that as this average pull-through rate goes up for the team, productivity for the group will be maximized.

The mistake with this approach is assuming each person has a similarly performing pipeline; in other words, every salesperson struggles with the same step in the sales process. Level 1 Coaches "generalize" and assume "one size fits all." Blanket performance statements are made about entire teams. In the sales example this could include comments such as "they are not good prospectors," "they don't ask enough questions to uncover needs," or "they are poor closers." While these are valid concerns and appropriate areas to focus on, they don't apply equally to each individual on the team. Managers must ***stop generalizing and start personalizing*** pipelines. The key is to quantify specific pull-through rates for each person and identify ailments that inhibit individual performance.

The situation of a doctor diagnosing a patient provides an excellent example about the importance of tailoring solutions to individual needs. Think how absurd it would be for an emergency room physician to generalize the needs of ALL patients based on the first situation he encountered that week. What if the first patient has acute appendicitis and the doctor performs an emergency appendectomy? Would you be excited to be the second patient? Imagine walking into the exam room to get some relief for an ear infection and the doctor immediately begins prepping you for surgery!

Too often, averages are used to judge performance. Managers reach for scalpels before they have done an adequate workup of what each person needs. Coaching efforts are generic and applied in a one-size-fits-all manner. The Level 1 Coach leaves the coaching session feeling good about her efforts, but the long-term impact is negligible because the coaching missed the target. In our medical example, the recovery room is loaded with patients that all had the same surgery even though they came in exhibiting very different symptoms.

In our work with sales leadership teams, we helped managers use existing reports to identify where the sales process broke down for each member of their team. Conversations shifted from inquiring about the status of individual deals to coaching skills at critical parts of the pipeline. When looking at the waterfall, or how many deals were at what stage of the pipeline, it became apparent where things got clogged. Once identified, QCC was utilized to assess why this was happening and to develop skills to overcome these challenges.

We reference the following table to illustrate this point.

	Leads Worked	Customer Contacts	Contact %	Apps Taken	App %	Customer Meetings	Meeting %	Deals Closed	Close %
Quinn	78	23	29%	12	52.2%	2	16.7%	2	100.0%
Shari	112	31	28%	11	35.5%	6	54.5%	0	0.0%
Rhonda	86	15	17%	8	53.3%	4	50.0%	2	50.0%
Miller	52	24	46%	13	54.2%	6	46.2%	0	0.0%
Kyle	89	27	30%	7	25.9%	3	42.9%	1	33.0%
Mason	104	26	25%	14	53.8%	7	50.0%	2	28.6%
Total	**521**	**146**		**65**		**28**		**5**	
Average	*86.8*	*24.3*	*29.3%*	*10.8*	*45.8%*	*4.7*	*43.4%*	*0.8*	*35.3%*

This hypothetical data represents ***one month of individual sales rep performance for each stage of the sales cycle***. While many conclusions can be reached from the data, our primary purpose is to demonstrate how performance must be evaluated at an individual level and not through team averages.

Let's focus on the bottom row of data in the table. These numbers represent ***average*** team performance at each stage of the pipeline. We took the liberty to outline five conclusions listed below: **(Note: These comparisons are made against hypothetical company performance standards shown in parentheses)**

1. Each salesperson worked an average of 86.8 leads for the month (10% above the company average.)
2. The customer contact rate for leads worked was 29.3% (12% below the company average.)
3. The team completed an application for 45.8% of contacts (8% above the company average.)
4. Of those customers for whom an application was taken, follow-up appointments were executed by the salespeople 43.4% of the time (2% below the company average.)
5. The close rate per salesperson was 35.3% (5% above the company average.)

Remember, this is fictitious data. The goal is not to judge whether the company benchmark performance metrics are good or bad. They are what they are. In addition, don't get hung up on this being a sales example if you work in a manufacturing environment. The same principles apply to whatever process or industry you happen to manage. Our goal is to understand how these numbers have the potential to lead you down the wrong path.

In this example, a likely conclusion is to improve Step 2, "increasing the customer contact rate." The numbers indicate performance in this section of the pipeline is below the company average. In fact, Step 2 has the greatest negative deviation from the average in comparison to the other steps. This conclusion ***appears*** to be clear cut. Improving customer contact rates for the team has to yield big results.

After you identify a process breakdown, it is time for action; in this case an all-out effort to improve customer contact rates for the team. As such, you place a singular focus on Step 2 of the process. Team meetings and conference calls are dedicated to the topic. Your QCC conversations focus on how each employee is going to improve his performance in this area. There isn't a day that goes by where you don't support this theme with words or action. It becomes a mantra for the quarter. It is an all-out assault to improve customer contact rates!

We have seen this phenomenom occur countless times in our work with organizations. Often these efforts yield minimal bottom line results, but why?

Let's take a closer look at the individual sales rep level for Step 2 of the process. The table below isolates performance at this specific step.

	Leads Worked	Customer Contacts	Contact %	Apps Taken	App %	Customer Meetings	Meeting %	Deals Closed	Close %
Quinn	78	23	29%	12	52.2%	2	16.7%	2	100.0%
Shari	112	31	28%	11	35.5%	6	54.5%	0	0.0%
Rhonda	86	15	17%	8	53.3%	4	50.0%	2	50.0%
Miller	52	24	46%	13	54.2%	6	46.2%	0	0.0%
Kyle	89	27	30%	7	25.9%	3	42.9%	1	33.0%
Mason	104	26	25%	14	53.8%	7	50.0%	2	28.6%
Total	**521**	**146**		**65**		**28**		**5**	
Average	*86.8*	*24.3*	*29.3%*	*10.8*	*45.8%*	*4.7*	*43.4%*	*0.8*	*35.3%*

Although the average customer contact rate is 29.3%, significant variation exists in terms of individual sales rep performance. In fact, the range from best to worst is 29%. Rhonda made contact with only 17% of her leads worked, while Miller successfully contacted 46% of his assigned leads. These two people are performing at different ends of the spectrum, which leads us to several important points.

First, more data is necessary. Accurate conclusions cannot be reached using only one data point. Additional data must be gathered to understand Normal and Special variation for this process. Simple rules of Statistical Process Control must be applied. Too often we overmanage by not understanding these principles. One piece of data does not make a trend. Miller's performance last month may have been very different from prior months. It is false to assume superstardom when looking at only his current month's results.

For simplicity's sake, let's assume these numbers accurately represent team performance from a historical perspective; Miller generally leads the team in customer contacts and Rhonda is consistently at the bottom. There is notable performance separation between them. Knowing this, we focus our attention on the manager's action outlined previously. How effective is it to have a universal focus on improving the team contact percentage?

The quick answer is, not very effective! This all-out blitz on improving customer contact rates for the team is off target. One cannot improve individual performance by driving a common theme across the team. It is similar to the emergency room doctor looking past individual patient symptoms. The needs of Rhonda and Miller are different. They are exhibiting different symptoms.

	Leads Worked	Customer Contacts	Contact %	Apps Taken	App %	Customer Meetings	Meeting %	Deals Closed	Close %
Quinn	78	23	29%	12	52.2%	2	16.7%	2	100.0%
Shari	112	31	28%	11	35.5%	6	54.5%	0	0.0%
Rhonda	86	15	17%	8	53.3%	4	50.0%	2	50.0%
Miller	52	24	46%	13	54.2%	6	46.2%	0	0.0%
Kyle	89	27	30%	7	25.9%	3	42.9%	1	33.0%
Mason	104	26	25%	14	53.8%	7	50.0%	2	28.6%
Total	**521**	**146**		**65**		**28**		**5**	
Average	*86.8*	*24.3*	*29.3%*	*10.8*	*45.8%*	*4.7*	*43.4%*	*0.8*	*35.3%*

Digging into Miller's performance measures illustrates the flawed logic at work. His performance is not being limited by how many customers he contacts. On the contrary, he leads the team in this area. His contact number is high, as is his contact percent. Improving this process yields nothing in terms of more booked business.

His performance is limited by a completely different step in the process. Coaching Miller in the area of contacts yields a poor ***Return on Time***.

According to the data, the limiting factor to Miller's sales performance is closing deals. Coaching him anywhere else in the process is wasted effort. One cannot manage to team averages. Doing so leads to wasted efforts and negligible results. Additional detail around this topic is provided later in this chapter.

Pipeline Paradigm #2 –Rarely Are Pipelines Shaped Like Funnels

The second paradigm to dispel is the misperception that pipelines are shaped like a traditional funnel; a wide mouth at the left, progressively getting smaller as you move to the right. We have been programmed to visualize pipelines this way as countless books depict them in this manner. However, in reality, pipelines rarely have this traditional shape.

Pipelines take on different shapes depending on the performance characteristics of the individual employee. The illustrations below represent a traditional view on the left, and an example of a personalized pipeline on the right.

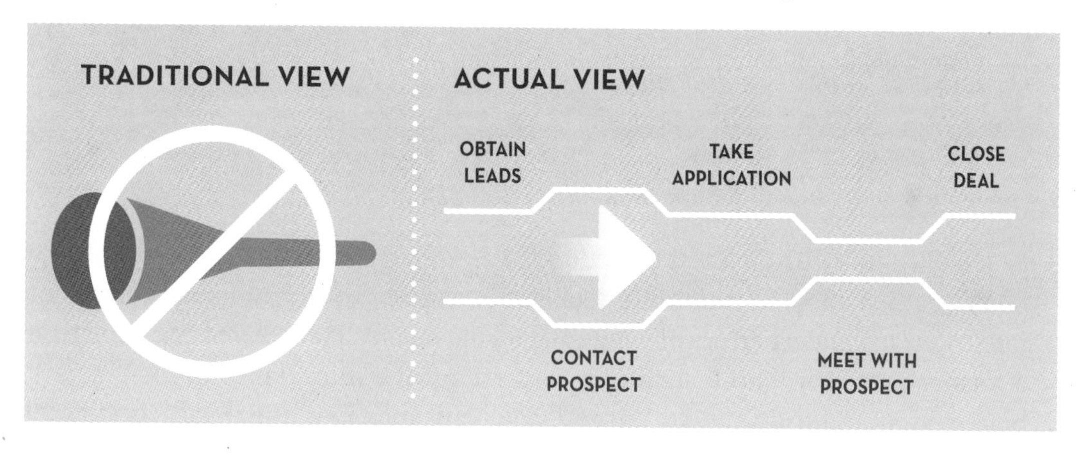

Assumptions associated with the traditional pipeline view are usually flawed. As represented in the actual view, pipelines are rarely perfectly formed funnels. Capacity varies throughout the cycle, independent of where the stage lies in the pipeline sequence. For example, salespeople operating in different markets, industries or economic environments have vastly different lead quantities available to pursue. For some, there are more leads to work than time available. For others, this section may be the limiting factor of their performance. Visually, these differences are represented through varied widths of the pipe.

It cannot be assumed that subsequent stages of the pipeline become narrower as you progress through the process. Execution of each stage varies by the individual.

It is not uncommon for later stages to be performed more effectively than earlier stages. For example, the pull through rate at stage 2 might be 45%, but the pull through rate at stage 3 is 75%. Just because it occurs later in the process doesn't mean that it has a lower pull through rate. Everyone's skills and natural talents uniquely align to the process, resulting in varied performance throughout. An effective coach understands that pipelines are often not shaped like a funnel, and before they start applying QCC it is important to understand where each employee has problems with his or her respective process.

Pipeline Paradigm #3 – Bottlenecks Limit Performance

The third pipeline paradigm is closely related to the second paradigm and involves understanding the significance of ***bottlenecks*** in relation to performance. Performance is limited by the bottleneck specific to each individual's respective pipeline. ***Focusing on non-bottleneck areas has no impact on bottom line results.***

KEY CONCEPT

Bottlenecks Limit Production

Dr. Eliyahu (Eli) Goldratt introduced the concept of bottlenecks in his 1986 book The Goal. This business tale details the struggles of a plant manager attempting to save his underperforming manufacturing facility. He received coaching from a former professor who helped him understand the importance of managing to bottlenecks or constraints. In the end, the plant manager utilized the bottleneck principal introduced by Dr. Goldratt to improve overall system performance and save the plant.

Paradigm #2 stressed the importance of visualizing pipelines in a non-traditional manner versus the traditional funnel. The image on the next page was used as an example of an actual sales pipeline.

Paradigm #3 builds on this image and focuses on the bottleneck, the section of the sales pipeline limiting overall production.

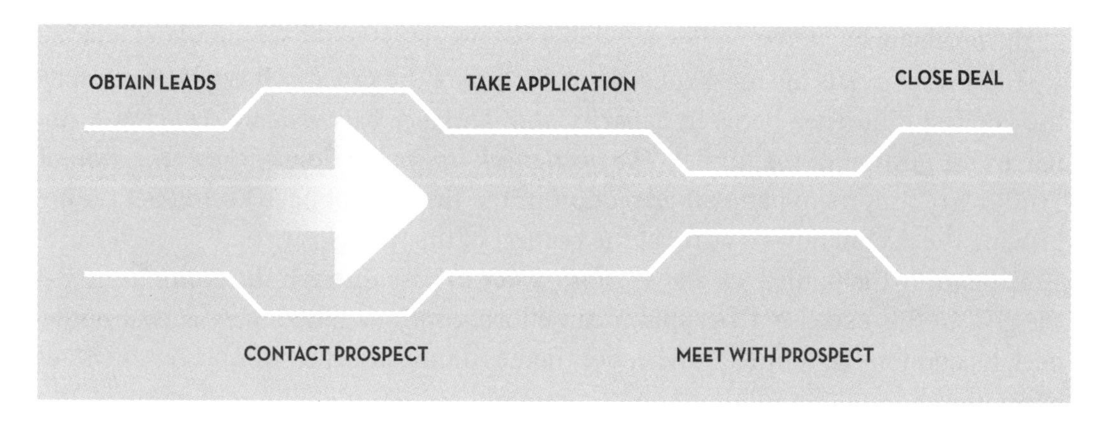

Pipeline metrics provide you directional data to accurately diagnose the needs of each individual on your team. A few questions to consider when identifying bottleneck locations include the following:

- At what stage does work fall out of the pipeline?
- Where do things consistently get bogged down?
- What part of the process is the individual least equipped to perform effectively?

These questions peel back the layers of generality and allow managers to hone in on specific challenges facing each individual.

The Water Funnel

The following illustration is the same pipeline rotated 90 degrees to offer a different perspective. This top-down flow provides a visual representation of the importance of working on the bottleneck in the system.

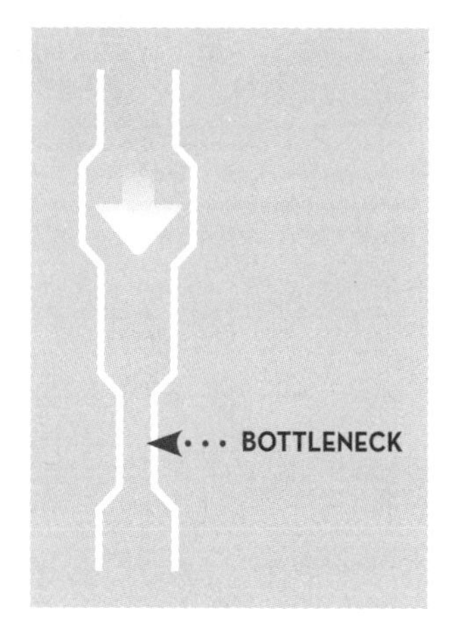

We use a simple example to illustrate this concept. Imagine pouring water through the funnel to the right. The goal is to increase the rate at which the water exits the bottom of the funnel. How is this best accomplished?

One option is to increase the rate at which water is poured into the top of the funnel. Unfortunately, this strategy is flawed. There is a limit to how much water the funnel can accept due to downstream constraints. The increased rate at the top of the funnel does not translate to an improved flow rate coming out the bottom. In addition to the goal not being met, the situation is worsened due to water overflowing the sides of the funnel. You create a real mess.

The optimal solution is to identify and expand the section constraining the water, or the ***bottleneck***.

This bottleneck is the most constricted section of the process. It is where you have the greatest difference between capacity and demand. It is visually depicted as the narrowest portion of the funnel. ***The bottleneck limits the flow of the entire funnel!*** Working on improving any other section in the funnel will have no impact on improving the overall flow of water at the bottom of the funnel.

Expanding the bottleneck allows more water to pass through the entire funnel — the goal in this exercise. Does that mean efforts continue indefinitely at that bottleneck location in the funnel? Maybe, but there is a time at which this becomes wasted effort as well.

As the original bottleneck expands, a point is reached where the overall flow becomes limited by a different section in the funnel; ***a new bottleneck***. Continued efforts at the original bottleneck become fruitless, and work must shift to the new constraint. Over time, a new constraint emerges, and the entire process is repeated yet again. This highlights how continuous improvement doesn't equate to *continuously working in the same place*.

So how does pouring water through an imaginary funnel relate to coaching employees? You might be surprised at the similarities. To illustrate this point, let's refer back to the data set referenced earlier in this chapter. Specifically, our focus now turns to the pipeline performance numbers for Quinn.

	Leads Worked	Customer Contacts	Contact %	Apps Taken	App %	Customer Meetings	Meeting %	Deals Closed	Close %
Quinn	78	23	29%	12	52.2%	2	16.7%	2	100.0%
Shari	112	31	28%	11	35.5%	6	54.5%	0	0.0%
Rhonda	86	15	17%	8	53.3%	4	50.0%	2	50.0%
Miller	52	24	46%	13	54.2%	6	46.2%	0	0.0%
Kyle	89	27	30%	7	25.9%	3	42.9%	1	33.0%
Mason	104	26	25%	14	53.8%	7	50.0%	2	28.6%
Total	**521**	**146**		**65**		**28**		**5**	
Average	*86.8*	*24.3*	*29.3%*	*10.8*	*45.8%*	*4.7*	*43.4%*	*0.8*	*35.3%*

The first step is to take the vertical water funnel pipeline depiction and overlay the steps from Quinn's process. In addition to representing a significant visual departure from the traditional funnel view, this also makes it clear that Quinn has a bottleneck at step 4, "Meet with Prospect."

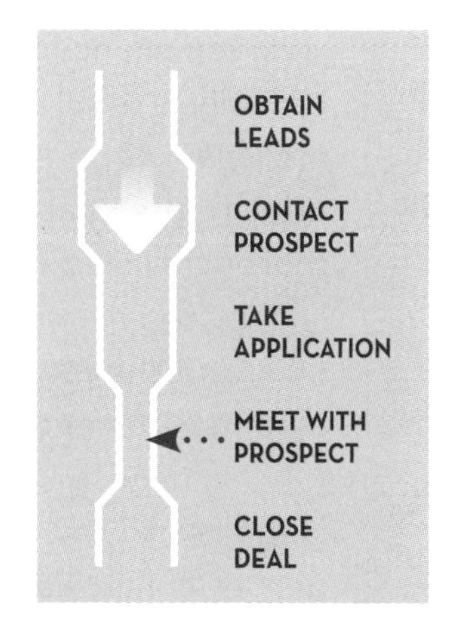

Quinn's performance depicts the following situation: adequate lead flow, successful contact with prospects, and a high percent of applications from those contacts. The bottleneck is step 4, which is "meet with prospect." Quinn's problem is getting customers to meet with him after he generates an application on the phone. When he meets face-to-face with customers, he has a high pull-through in regard to closed deals.

The same strategies apply to Quinn's pipeline as those outlined with the water funnel. If Quinn's manager invested time working at Step 1, increasing lead flow, what would be the result? Based on what we know, the rate at which deals close would not improve. This activity is similar to pouring water in faster at the top of the funnel. In this case, the negative consequence is not water spilling over the sides, but a clogged pipeline with more opportunities stuck inside. The goal is not to get more in; it is to get more out!

Pouring in more water actually leads to a negative investment and is costly in numerous ways. In this example, "pouring more leads" into Quinn's funnel wastes resources or leads that cannot be converted and takes opportunity away from other members of the team.

To reiterate a previous point, the manager feels like he executed a successful coaching session, but his impact was detrimental because he focused on the wrong part of the process!

This is an oversimplified example. In this scenario, numerous variables affect where bottlenecks might be in the pipeline: changing market conditions, product demand, pricing, etc. What doesn't change is the importance of targeted coaching activities based on salesperson needs. As one constraint is broken, others emerge. ***Today's solutions are tomorrow's problems!***

A Personal Experience – Coaching to Non-Bottleneck Areas

We frequently observed managers misfiring on their coaching efforts due to a poor diagnosis of the pipeline. They simply worked in the wrong part of the process, in non-bottleneck areas, from what the data indicated. They didn't take time to properly diagnose where the process was breaking down.
The situation described above was commonplace, but I encountered a slightly different scenario that stood out from all the others. I was traveling with a

very experienced area manager, and we were observing a coaching session between a retail site manager and one of her employees. In this case, the site manager properly diagnosed the pipeline clog. She had done her homework prior to the coaching session. She ran productivity reports, reviewed them thoroughly, and then accurately determined which step in the process was limiting the employee's performance. We sat down prior to the coaching session, and she reviewed her diagnosis with the area manager and me. We all agreed with her assessment and looked forward to the coaching session.

Needless to say, I was extremely impressed with the solid preparation and proper diagnosis. It was perfect; if only every manager prepared like this! What happened next was what made this noteworthy.

The coaching conversation quickly veered off course. The manager and employee honed in on areas different than what were diagnosed as problems. When it came time to develop specific actions, the agreed-upon activities focused on a part of the process that was performing well, not the bottleneck! In other words, the diagnosis was spot on, but the actions were 100% off target! The manager focused her coaching efforts on the "Close," but this particular salesperson "Closed" very well. The problem for this salesperson was that she simply didn't have enough opportunities in the pipeline, the true need and place requiring attention. Ironically, the manager reverted back to a stand-by solution instead of developing something new that addressed the specific needs of the individual.

This is yet another example of how difficult it is to break old habits. It also reiterates the importance of managers coaching to the right part of the process. Coaching must be targeted to individual needs. It is paramount to creating manager leverage.

CLOSING THOUGHT

The pipeline is a powerful tool for managers to identify where to coach each member of her team. Performance pipelines rarely take on the shape of a traditional funnel. Thinking of them in this manner is misleading. Pipelines must be personalized to each individual based on his or her performance. Doing so highlights the differing needs of each person, leading to more customized coaching. The most significant benefit of personalizing pipelines is the ability to identify the bottleneck. Bottlenecks are the step in the process that have the greatest difference between capacity and demand. Working anywhere in the process, other than at the constraint, yields limited results.

CALL TO ACTION

- ❑ Create a high level process map depicting how work flows through your team and/or organization.
- ❑ Identify existing reports that measure individual performance and align them against this process.
- ❑ Analyze the reports to identify bottlenecks for each member of your team.
- ❑ Evaluate prior coaching efforts with each team member to determine whether your efforts are focused on the bottleneck.
- ❑ Prepare a list of questions prior to your next coaching session that focus on the bottleneck. Refer back to Chapter 7 to include questions from each of the Strategic Question Categories (Diagnostic, Satisfaction, Sizing, and Resolution).
- ❑ Work with the individual being coached to determine how to measure improvement in the bottleneck area.

Chapter 10
Coaching to Strengths and Being Prepared

Chapter 9 explored the first of the three core elements of how to execute QCC. Specifically, the last chapter focused on the importance of using the pipeline as a tool to identify where to coach. Pipelines must be personalized to each individual on your team. It is critical that you identify and coach to individual bottlenecks. This is very different than applying generic coaching to the entire team with a "one size fits all" approach.

KEY CONCEPT

Core Elements of How to Execute QCC

1. *Identifying Where to Coach*
2. *Coaching to Strengths*
3. *Being Prepared*

Chapter 10 explores the second and third critical elements of how to execute QCC: coaching to individual strengths, and the importance of being thoroughly prepared.

Coaching to Individual Strengths

Each member of your team is unique. Individuals are wired differently and bring distinctive talents, strengths, and experiences to their role. Level 3 Coaches recognize and leverage these unique talents with each member of their team.

Benson Smith and Tony Ritigliano eloquently articulate these points in their book *Discover Your Sales Strengths.* The book is based on their extensive research while working for the Gallup Organization and emphasizes the need for managers to understand how each member of their team is motivated, evaluates situations, builds relationships, influences others, and organizes and executes their work. A Level 3

Coach helps his employees maximize their talents and develop an authentic style or brand. You need to stop trying to make people into what you think they should be and instead focus on helping them accentuate what makes them uniquely good.

The last chapter spoke to the importance of targeting your coaching efforts on bottleneck processes. Understanding where the pipeline is clogged for each member of your team is critical, but this only tells where to coach, not how to coach.

A common misstep Level 1 Coaches make is to force every member of their team to perform processes exactly the same way. While it is important to establish a defined process from which the team operates, it cannot come at the expense of nullifying individual strengths. These two elements are not mutually exclusive; members of your team can execute a common process while exhibiting personal flair based on their unique blend of strengths. Leveraging personal strengths in the process creates greater authenticity, elevates performance, and increases employee engagement.

Assume you are coaching an employee on ways to build relationships and establish credibility. You both agree it is essential he improve his credibility with a key internal client; without establishing credibility with this individual, it will be difficult for him to be successful in his role.

You happen to be very confident and have an outgoing and gregarious personality that wins people over. This style is very natural to you, and you use this approach to quickly form relationships and establish credibility; it has been a key to your success over the years.

When coaching others you quickly defer to what works for you. In this case, your coaching focuses on changing the personality of your team member, having them take on attributes that made you successful. You focus on what he needs to say, how to say it, and what worked for you when you were in that role. The problem with this approach is that it ignores the specific traits of the individual being coached.

Not all successful relationship builders possess glowing personalities. That is okay, as there are other strengths in which a person can call upon to achieve credibility. One of the most effective client relationship managers we worked with fits this description. He is not someone you would describe as being the life of the party or the person customers want to go have a drink with. Simply stated, he doesn't have that glowing "sales" personality. What he does have is an extremely strategic and analytical approach to his job, and one that lends itself to establishing credibility. When he speaks, people listen. In fact, they can't wait to hear him speak because he knows more about the industry and more about his customer's business than anyone else. He builds trust by knowing the right questions to ask and possessing thought leadership that is an invaluable resource to those around him.

Now let's tie this example back to coaching. Assume you are a manager and a person with these strengths joins your team. An analysis of their pipeline highlights a bottleneck that underscores a problem in establishing rapport and building credibility. How would you coach this person?

Unfortunately, too many managers revert to a "personality changing" tactic. They try to get people to become something they are not. They coax the employee to use the same style that made them successful back in their days of occupying that same job. We profess taking a different approach, coaching individuals based on their unique strengths. In this case, the outstanding thinking strengths of the relationship manager. Getting him to develop a natural way to leverage his analytical skills would be a much more rewarding approach; for the manager and the employee. The employee will feel better about doing what comes natural to him, and the manager will get a more engaged and productive employee.

A Personal Experience – Coaching to Strengths

My career has offered me the unique and rewarding opportunity to work with talented people across many industries, organizations and professional disciplines. Through this work I have come to appreciate how successful people find ways to bring a personal flair to their roles. They leverage their personal strengths to be successful. This requires a manager who respects these individual differences and coaches to employee strengths.

One particular situation involved a woman struggling to be successful in life insurance sales. Her success was dependent on how effectively she identified prospects, made contact, cultivated relationships, and earned enough trust to sell her products. Her work required a thick skin, as she received a lot of "no thanks" when making cold calls.

She had an underwriting background, so she was extremely knowledgeable about her products, and was a true technician of the industry. Few could rival her knowledge, strategic thinking ability, or her analytical mind. Unfortunately, her sales results were not good.

I was contacted by her manager, who asked if I could provide him with some suggestions on how he could help improve her performance. He was extremely frustrated with her results, and although he had invested time to help her get better, his efforts did not yield measurable results.

I scheduled a meeting with the manager to understand what, where, and how he was coaching the woman. I asked multiple questions, all of which were written down prior to our meeting. My questions followed our strategic process outlined in Chapter 7, and included questions from each of the four categories: Diagnostic, Satisfaction, Sizing, and Resolution. It was important to model the behavior I expected him to utilize when coaching.

From our conversation, it became apparent that his "coaching" approach was very different than what we have described throughout this book. He did a lot of telling; he pushed ideas on the her. He asked very few questions, and when he did, his intention was to find fault. Most importantly, and the point of this story, he was telling her things to do that were contrary to her natural talents. His goal was to get her to use the same techniques that worked for him when he was a salesperson. This included shaking hands and gathering business cards at community networking events and parties, speaking at chamber meetings and breakfast clubs, and finding any way to get in front of more people. The problem was that she was not flashy or outgoing, and it was difficult to find prospects that were a good fit for her style.

My suggestion was to take a different approach. I asked him about her strengths, and more importantly, how we could get her connected with other prospects that would appreciate her deliberate and analytical approach. Through my questions, the manager came to several great ideas, which ultimately yielded significant results.

The most significant change focused on where and who she prospected. The manager aligned her to people who relied on a pragmatic thinking style. This included accountants, chief financial officers, underwriters, engineers, and scientists. Rather than changing her, the manager changed her targeted clientele, which was a simple, but powerful, adjustment.

QCC capitalizes on the natural talents of the person being coached. Leverage is expanded as conversations are tailored to the dynamic needs and talents of each person on the team. To reiterate a concept from Chapter 5, effective coaches focus on the input side of the process model shown on the next page. In the previous story, the key input was who the women targeted when prospecting for new clients.

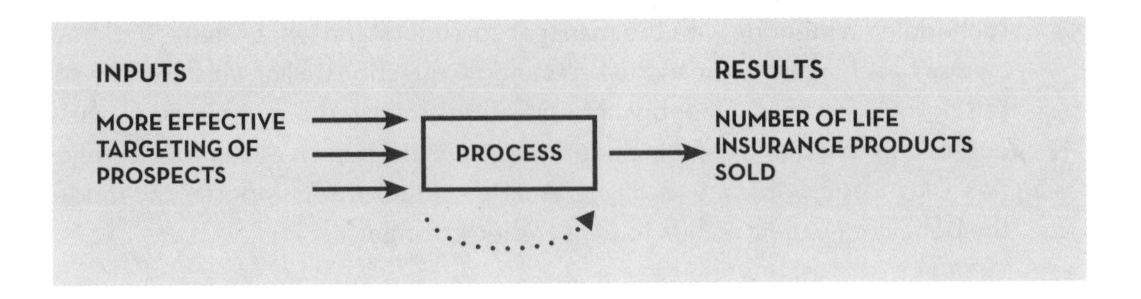

Discussions are predicated by current obstacles facing the individual. This could include challenges with an internal or external client, changing processes or economic pressures, or a myriad of other unique needs. Coaching evolves over time as needs change. This dynamic quality is what makes QCC conversations so valuable! Responses to questions allow the individual being coached to develop critical thinking skills, improve productivity, and for you to gain system insight and improve leverage.

Being Thoroughly Prepared

Thorough preparation is the third factor related to the successful deployment of QCC. QCC is not a strategy that bodes well if you are the type of manager who flies by the seat of your pants. Being ill-prepared for coaching conversations will undermine your QCC and lead to lackluster results.

The importance of adequate preparation is interwoven throughout the coaching process. You must avoid getting sucked back "in" the system and develop a defined coaching plan. Absence of a plan leaves much to chance and diminishes the likelihood that key coaching activities will actually take place. Time must be spent preparing a coaching plan for the upcoming week and month. However, establishing a plan is only part of the equation. Successful QCC execution requires consistent preparation in other areas as well.

To illustrate how preparation impacts coaching execution, we refer to the Coaching Conversation Process introduced in Chapter 5.

We spoke to the importance of predictability in terms of how coaching conversations are performed. Precious time is wasted when a person comes into a coaching discussion with you not knowing what to expect. When you execute coaching conversations leveraging a consistent model, you get the power of predictability working in your favor. The following model was introduced as a means to achieve predictability.

Preparedness on the part of you and your employee is a key to effective execution of the model. This preparedness begins with the first step, "Review Prior Commitments." If you come into a coaching conversation without adequate preparation, you leave opportunities on the table.

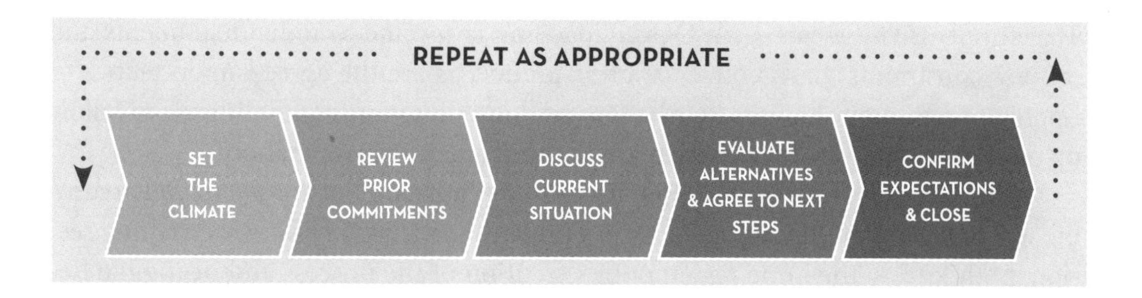

Lack of preparation manifests itself when you ignore previous actions agreed-upon by your team member. Instead, discussions focus on new challenges and opportunities. Although important, this can't occur at the expense of reviewing prior commitments. Both elements must be covered.

Poor follow-up sends the message that prior QCC conversations are not important, eroding the impact of future coaching sessions. The net result is you having the same conversations over and over again; the ultimate waste of resources. It is amazing how often this occurs.

Having awareness around this problem is a good first step, but effective problem solvers understand the importance of identifying causes before generating solutions. Why something happens is critical before determining how to fix it. There are two prevalent causes of why this step is so often skipped.

First, you assume too much about your employees when it comes to changing behavior. You give individuals the benefit of the doubt and assume activities will automatically improve following a single QCC conversation. The prevailing mindset is if you coach to an issue, conformance will automatically follow. If it were only that easy!

No, there isn't a conspiracy by your team to secretly defy strategies you mutually developed. You are working against the forces of momentum and how things have always been done. Creating personal change is very difficult. Even with the best intentions it is difficult to change behavior. Doing so requires the coach to follow up on prior commitments by asking well-directed questions.

The second cause of poor follow-up is your lack of preparation prior to a coaching conversation with an employee. There are considerable demands on your time, both planned and unplanned. You constantly have to react to an onslaught of urgent issues. Your calendar is packed full of conference calls and meetings, one after another. This urgency creates bad habits, one of the worst being poor preparation for meetings.

You may argue your performance doesn't suffer from poor preparation; you are smart enough to "think on your feet" and quickly "shift gears" to the topic at hand.

That simply isn't the case with QCC. Coaching is specific to individual talents and process constraints. Each conversation is unique, as are the agreed-upon tactics to improve performance. No matter how good you think you are, it's difficult to follow up on the assortment of coaching plans without adequate preparation.

Whether the cause of poor follow-up to prior commitments is due to you assuming too much about the employee, or not preparing adequately for the coaching session, both lead to the same result: poor execution of the process and negligible Return on Time.

The solution to this problem is not complex. Step one requires you to prepare for QCC conversations by reviewing previous commitments. Simple as that! Investing time reviewing notes from the last discussion pays big dividends. The second step is to write down questions for the conversation to follow up on those commitments. Don't leave this to chance. Spend a few minutes identifying good questions that adhere to the strategic question model introduced in Chapter 8. For each commitment, be prepared to ask Diagnostic, Satisfaction, Sizing, and Resolution questions.

We can hear you now, "I don't have time to prepare questions like this." Again we offer a simple solution. Develop a standard series of questions that can be applied universally to different scenarios. This provides a dual benefit of reducing preparation time and increasing predictability.

Below is a suggested series of questions to follow up on prior commitments. We recommend you personalize them to your style and comfort, as these are intended to function as suggestions and not scripts.

These same questions can be used repeatedly in QCC discussions without customization. They are universal and apply to any follow-up conversation.

KEY CONCEPT

Follow-Up Questions on Prior Commitments

1. *Describe the changes you made following our last meeting?*
2. *How did this change affect your performance?*
3. *Are things better? Is it worth continuing?*
4. *What was the impact on your results?*
5. *What help do you need from me?*

Your preparation is critical. The distribution of talk time should favor those being coached. You must ask good questions and be a good listener. The goal is for you to ask questions and let the individual being coached do the majority of the talking. The objective is to have the employee accountable for his actions, not vice versa.

This leads to another suggestion as it relates to transferring ownership of action items from the manager to the employee. As a manager, resist the temptation to recap the conversation for the individual being coached. Instead, have your team member provide a written recap of the meeting to you. Doing so transfers the burden from you to them, exactly where it should be! Although subtle, this change is significant. Doing so takes a tremendous burden off of the manager in terms of having to know exactly where each conversation will begin.

CLOSING THOUGHT

The pipeline is a powerful tool for managers to identify where to coach each member of their team. Pipelines must be personalized to each individual based on her performance. Doing so highlights the differing needs of each person, leading to more customized coaching.

When coaching to bottlenecks, QCC focuses on an individual's strengths. The goal is to understand how the strengths of each individual align to the process in which they work. Your role is to help people develop an authentic style based on their natural talents.

QCC requires preparation by both parties. Lack of preparation by you sends the message that the process is not that important. More importantly, lack of preparation reduces the effectiveness of the conversation and erodes the impact of your efforts.

CALL TO ACTION

- ❑ Take time to reflect on the unique strengths and talents of your direct report team. Write down attributes that make them unique. Consider how they think, build relationship, and influence others. Ask them what motivates and inspires them to higher performance.
- ❑ For each individual, evaluate how effectively he incorporates his unique talents into his role. Also, consider how you manage and coach members of your team to leverage these strengths more frequently.
- ❑ Have your employee provide you with a brief recap of changes he plans to implement following your next coaching session.
- ❑ Use the follow-up questions outlined on page 94 to review progress against those stated actions.

Chapter 11
Executing "On" vs. "In"

A key concept of this book is for you to recognize the importance of working "on" versus "in" the system and to know the types of activities that fall in each category. We identified situations where you need to strategically work "in" the system to gain greater knowledge and improve your ability to apply the principles of QCC. We stressed the importance of moving back to a position of working "on" the system after your deliberate and temporary work "in" the system.

Our goal in this chapter is to help you learn how to execute the "on" versus "in" strategy. Ultimately, QCC cannot be effectively deployed if you reduce your leverage by working "in" the system.

KEY CONCEPT

To maximize employee learning, Level 3 Coaches utilize QCC to review the plan prior to a meeting in which they lead for demonstration purposes.

Having a game plan and identifying desired outcomes is important when going into any meeting. Preparation is even more important when you use this type of situation to demonstrate the proper way to run a meeting for an employee. Below are questions you could ask an employee prior to leading such a discussion:

- How should we approach this group and begin the conversation?

- How do you recommend we articulate our value proposition?

- What are the specific needs of the team?
  - ▹ *How do you know?*
  - ▹ *What risk do we face if we haven't identified all of their needs?*
  - ▹ *Would it be helpful if we created additional questions to identify needs?*

- How will the group benefit from engaging with us?
  - ▹ *Do they experience problems with their current process?*
  - ▹ *What types of problems?*
  - ▹ *How do these issues impact their group?*

- What objections should we anticipate?
  - ▹ *How do you propose we respond?*

- What is our desired outcome of the meeting?
  - ▹ *What do we "ask" for at the conclusion of this meeting?*
  - ▹ *What is the impact if they don't agree to this?*
  - ▹ *What is our fallback objective?*

Just because you are taking the lead and your employee isn't driving the agenda shouldn't cause you to skip the pre-meeting coaching questions. A lot can be learned from observation if the person observing knows specifically what to look for. A back-up quarterback in football prepares for a game exactly the same as the starter. They don't sit around without any responsibility. The same is true in industry. Asking your team questions forces them to think and prepare as if they were taking the lead. Not asking questions allows them to sit back with few responsibilities and the likelihood of learning diminishes significantly.

KEY CONCEPT

To maximize employee learning, Level 3 Coaches ask questions following a meeting in which they lead for demonstration purposes.

- How do you feel the meeting went?
  - ▹ *What went well?*
  - ▹ *What didn't go well? Why?*
  - ▹ *What do you think we could have done differently?*

- How was rapport established with the other party?
  - ▹ *Was it effective?*
  - ▹ *What impact did establishing that level of rapport have on the conversation?*
  - ▹ *Would it have been helpful to ask additional questions?*
  - ▹ *If yes, what questions do you suggest?*

- Who did more talking; me or them?
  - ▹ *Did I ask more questions or make more statements?*
  - ▹ *How did this impact the meeting?*
  - ▹ *Do you feel it changed the outcome of the conversation?*

- How well did I articulate our Value Proposition?

- Describe how I confirmed their high-value needs.
  - ▹ *Why is that important?*
  - ▹ *How did this impact the discussion?*

- What objections did you hear from the other party?
  - ▹ *How did I respond to those objections?*
  - ▹ *Was that effective?*
  - ▹ *What could I have done differently?*

- What do you see as the next steps or follow-up from today's meeting?
  - ▹ *What is the best way to ask this?*
  - ▹ *What do you think their reaction will be?*
  - ▹ *How do you suggest we move forward if they react a different way?*

Conversations with employees before and after demonstrating a key process is a key to effective coaching. These conversations are in real time and around real issues. There is nothing theoretical about them. Coaching situations like this are vital to developing the thinking skills necessary for your employees to be successful. The intent of this process is to transfer knowledge in addition to completing the activity.

Leading a meeting in place of your employee is a prime example of working "in" the system. However, adjusting the process by asking pre- and post-meeting questions shifts this activity to that of working "on" the system; a minor adjustment, but one that reaps big benefits to you and your team member.

How to Avoid Getting Sucked Back into the System

Change is hard! It is difficult for managers to move from working "in" the system to working "on" the system. Reaching that vantage point takes focus and self-discipline. Once there, the perch is equally difficult to maintain. Old habits die hard.

Reality TV is all the rage at the time of writing this book and the show called "The Biggest Loser" ranks high in popularity. The program features eighteen contestants who enter the program overweight and looking to change their eating and exercise habits. The motivation to undergo this extreme mental and physical challenge is varied, but a prevalent reason cited is the desire "to be around for their loved ones." The participants don't want a life cut short by their bad habits to negatively impact those they care most about.

Amazing transformations occur over 10 weeks. Diets radically change. Regimented exercise becomes the norm. Hundreds of pounds are shed. Winners lose nearly fifty percent of their body weight! Remarkable makeovers happen in front of the audience's eyes.

The reason for referencing this show is simple. Many participants share the concern when they go home they will fall back into old habits; even with the positive outcomes associated with losing weight, fear about getting "sucked" back into bad habits remains! Everyone recognizes how perilous this position is.

Changing personal habits is extremely hard. In fact, some sources say it takes at least twenty-one continuous days of not performing a bad habit to break it. If it were easy, new fad diets wouldn't be created every year to get people to lose the "same" weight they lost the year before. People are creatures of habit. Changing behaviors

KEY CONCEPT

It is just as difficult to maintain new habits as it is to break old ones!

requires knowledge, a plan, and consistent reinforcement. Habits, good or bad, fill a void. Part of breaking a bad habit is filling the void created when the habit is stopped. You need a plan and reinforcement to be successful.

Changing organizational habits is equally difficult. Inertia is a powerful force operating inside businesses. People don't know what they don't know. Infusing a coaching culture into an entity void of that mentality requires new and persuasive knowledge to offset the "this is how we've always done it" mentality. Following is a real-world example.

A Personal Experience - Changing Organizational Behavior

In an early engagement, we were challenged with the task of improving the performance of a 100+ person national sales force that called on Auto Dealers. Regional salespeople were assigned to make sales calls to all the dealers in their territory. Their ultimate goal was to sign new dealers that did not already represent the company and improve sales volume with dealers previously contracted.

As with all engagements, we started by asking a lot of questions; in this case to the regional salespeople with whom we were partnering to improve performance. Our questions focused on how they constructed their days and included the following:

- When do you start visiting dealers?
- How many dealers do you visit in a day?
- How do you determine what dealership to call on?
- Who do you talk to in a dealership? Why?
- What is the expected outcome of your visit?
- How do you prepare for your visit?
- When do you call on existing dealerships versus prospective dealerships?
- How much time do you spend with each dealer?
- What is your definition of success?
- Based on your definition of success, who is doing well, who is lagging?
- What are the best practices?

Our questions yielded some interesting answers. We found little consistency in preparation, definition of success, or expected outcomes as a result of a meeting with a dealer. We did find a common practice of meeting with all dealers in an assigned territory once a month. In essence, this became the driving force behind scheduling. Sales reps would drive past three dealerships with substantial opportunity to get to one dealer with very small revenue opportunity just because they "had to show up once per month."

Prior to our interviews, the sales manager gave us a list of producers in descending order of sales volume. One of the "problems" the manager wanted to "fix" was five out of the top seven performing salespeople did not keep with the requirement of visiting all assigned dealerships monthly. Because these five top salespeople performed so well, the manager felt like he could not "get on these people" since he did not want to alienate the top producers. This was in spite of the fact that they were setting a bad example for the rest of the team by not "following the rules" and visiting each dealership every month.

We also interviewed the sales manager. Where did the "visitation rule" come from? He had created it. What was the purpose of the rule? "To make sure salespeople see dealers."

After a few more interviews, it became obvious that what the team needed was a better targeting strategy than "see each dealer every month." On what basis should salespeople prioritize their clients and prospects? We asked each sales rep to plot each dealer against two axis: Volume Opportunity and Market Share. The Volume Opportunity, or x-axis, measured total sales volume for the dealer. This reflected how many cars the dealer sold each month. A large dealer selling lots of cars represents a bigger opportunity for the sales rep. The Market Share, or y-axis, measured how much Volume the sales rep captured from the dealer.

We formed a 2 x 2 matrix that quickly showed where the opportunity for new volume existed. The 'Opportunity Targeting' model is shown below:

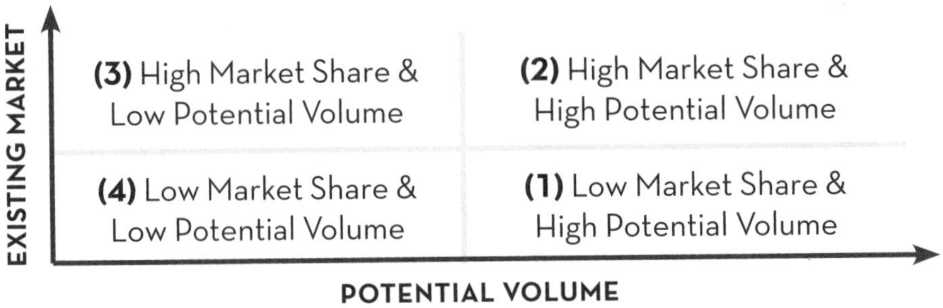

EXISTING MARKET ↑		
	(3) High Market Share & Low Potential Volume	**(2)** High Market Share & High Potential Volume
	(4) Low Market Share & Low Potential Volume	**(1)** Low Market Share & High Potential Volume
	POTENTIAL VOLUME →	

Below is an overview of the types of dealers found in each box of the 2 x 2 matrix.

Box 1 = These customers present a fun opportunity, and next year's bonus potentially resides here. This customer generates significant volume, yet your market penetration is low. There is a lot of opportunity available, and it would be wise to develop a plan to grow market share.

Box 2 = These customers love you! They typically pay on time and make great references. You might need to adjust your relationship strategy, as the opportunity is currently maximized. It is critical to maintain this important customer relationship.

Box 3 = You need to be careful that you don't get too consumed with these customers. You currently receive the majority of their business, but it is a limited opportunity. This is a great customer, but not enough to live on.

Box 4 = You need to ask yourself, why am I spending time with this customer? These customers offer low opportunity, even with increased market share. Rethink why you are investing time with this customer. If an appropriate opportunity exists, work hard and win the business. If not, run away.

Based on analysis from this simple model, the sales manager quickly recalibrated his thinking, shared the data with his sales team, and developed account sales and servicing strategies that were much more consistent with the actual goals of the organization. The new strategy was also consistent with what we viewed as informal best practices already in use by the top salespeople.

This example demonstrates how powerful organizational inertia can be and how powerful questions can be in changing individual habits. We spoke previously about how habits fill a void. Breaking the habit of seeing every dealer (and in essence, considering each as an equal opportunity) in the territory would not have happened without a proven strategy to replace this thinking.

The likelihood is strong that you were promoted into your position because you were the top individual performer on the team. While this is a common practice, it is not without its faults. For example, there is no rule that states a top accountant will automatically make a good accounting manager, or a top salesperson will automatically be a high-performing sales leader. In fact, many attributes that led to success for a person as an individual contributor often inhibits his success in management. We are not implying it can't be done, but the transition is not nearly as natural as one would expect. In fact, the difficulty in transitioning from a successful technical contributor to an effective manager of people is a consistent theme across many professional disciplines.

The accolades and satisfaction received from consistently outperforming co-workers is often greater than the less alluring reward of leading a team to greatness. The primary activities performed as a leader are different than those performed as an individual contributor. The focus and drive to achieve personal results don't always translate into the ability to develop the talents of team members, especially those who have differing personalities and strengths when compared to your own.

Don't get us wrong. We are not implying that you should not consider promoting your top people into leadership roles. In the world of accounting, it is doubtful you will experience success by taking technology specialists and making them your chief financial officer. Up-and-coming accounting and finance people are frequently the best source of talent to fill the CFO pipeline. However, plucking talent from this pipeline and inserting them into key management roles without consideration and development of their coaching skills is a costly mistake. Following are two personal experiences: one where it worked, and one where it didn't.

A Personal Experience - Hiring the Wrong Sales Manager

Early in my career, I led a high-performing group of hard-charging Business to Business salespeople. These people called on executives of financial institutions across the country. As a team, we were very successful.

Our continued success in contracting with more financial institutions created a need to expand our team. This meant more executive level salespeople and another regional sales manager. Our top performing salesperson, let's call him Bob, was "all over me" about not only being considered, but having "already earned" the new sales manager role. While he never said it, leaving the company to join the competition was a real possibility if Bob didn't get the position.

I was the youngest senior sales leader in our company. Bob was the highest-performing salesperson in the company. We weren't going to lose Bob on my watch! I took the easy way out, made the "obvious decision," and promoted Bob....what a disaster!

To be clear, it was not a disaster because Bob was a top-performing salesperson. It was a disaster because Bob was a terrible fit for the new position. What the company and regional sales team needed, Bob did not have.

Bob's ego "demanded" he get the job. What the sales team needed was a coach; someone that could grow the capacity, knowledge, skills, and confidence of the individuals under his or her leadership; someone that could ask the right questions and guide the team.

Bob was a driver. He drove himself hard and the team harder. Bob had low patience. Everything came easy for Bob, and he had no tolerance for people that needed real coaching. I had made a real mess. My most productive salesperson was now "out of production," and, worse than that, he was causing other above-average people to consider leaving the company since Bob was so difficult to work with. Not good!

In the end, I was lucky. Bob realized he was not "in his element." I was able to help him understand that simply telling someone what to do does not guarantee results or make one a leader. We previously spoke about three coaching levels. Bob was a classic Level 1 Coach. His ego demanded he be #1, and the quickest road to that was going back into the field. Once we pulled that off, the world was a better place.

Learning from Mistakes

A few years later, it was time to hire another sales manager because the incumbent was retiring. This time we did a better job. We had the luxury of time, so we carefully thought through the needs of the sales organization and the individual sales performers that would be on the new manager's team. I asked myself what were the 3 to 5 key things the sales team needed in a new regional manager. I'm not talking about the job description. I mean over the next 12 to 24 months, what were the few things that this team needed most to get to the next level of performance? Then I did something radical! I asked the sales team the same questions. (It is amazing what you can do with questions!) Asking the team was really beneficial as it helped round out some of the perceived needs.

Now we were on cruise control. I knew what we needed. Not just a successful salesperson but a respected member of the team that was dialed in to both the emerging trends in the market and to the skill gap of the team in comparison to where the market was going. We needed this person to identify where our team was currently stalled.

> At the end of the process, it was not only clear to me, but to the broader team who was the best fit. We hired a respected salesperson that ranked sixth out of twenty people in sales volume. Because we spent time up front analyzing the needs of the team, when Jill took over she rapidly became a Level 3 Coach. She led her team to record success, not by giving orders, but by coaching. She asked questions, determined needs, gained agreement and followed up. Jill held her team accountable and the team responded. No mystery, no over-blown ego. Jill had never led a team of this nature before, but we both knew she would be successful even before she started her new role.

The same is true in regard to working "on" the system. It is not easy to maintain that focus when momentum wants to pull you back "in." We've found four keys for leaders to avoid being sucked back "in" the system.

KEY CONCEPT

How to Avoid Being Sucked Back "in" the System

1. Have a Plan

2. Execute the Plan

3. Minimize Upward Delegation

4. Define your Accessibility

1. Have a Plan – When you come into the day, week, or month without a plan, you put yourself at great risk of being sucked back "in" the system. When operating without a plan, you react to the first thing that comes your way. You are susceptible to having miscellaneous e-mails or phone calls set the course for your day; a surefire way to stay busy, but not the road to success.

Very few people in corporate America aren't busy. Everyone is being asked to do more with less. Being busy is not the issue. Being effective and developing a powerful plan is the issue. Too often, you allow urgency to monopolize importance.

One of our mentors uses a great statement to emphasize the importance of having a plan: "It is difficult to execute blank." Not only is it difficult to execute blank, but blank creates an environment where focus is easily diverted to whatever happens to pop up on a given day.

Don't misinterpret the phrase "having a plan" as a need for complexity. A coaching plan can be simple as long as it answers the following questions for you:

- Who is going to get my time this week, month, quarter?
- How much time is necessary for each individual? Why?
- When do they need my time? Is it time-sensitive?
- Where is the process breaking down? Where is the bottleneck?
- What specifically are we trying to accomplish together?
- How will we measure progress?
- How will they prepare?
- How will I prepare?
- How will we measure success?

A common misperception is that each member of a team requires equal coaching time. In reality, each employee has different needs, requiring unique strategies and investments of time. All things are not created equal when it comes to allocating time to coaching.

Having a coaching plan on paper is one thing. Having a coaching plan that is embedded in the daily execution of managerial duties is another. The key is for you to integrate coaching into your daily activities and not view it as something separate and disconnected from your job. Coaching is part of your job.

An essential tool to bring a plan to life is also one of the simplest: a calendar. Whether it is housed on an electronic handheld device, a Franklin Planner, or a cocktail napkin is not relevant. You must develop a system that works for you and stick to it. Plan your work and work your plan.

Your calendar must support your coaching plan and what you are trying to accomplish, bringing your plan to life through a disciplined approach around critical daily activities.

Take a moment to review your calendar for the upcoming week. Is your time allocated to working "in" the system or "on" the system? Do you have time blocked on your calendar for QCC, one of the most important "on" system activities, or is your calendar filled with conference calls, meetings, and personal appointments?

Is your goal to try and fit coaching in when you have time and your day is not filled with other activities? Unfortunately, that is not an effective plan as those well-intentioned discussions rarely take place. Your time is consumed with unplanned emergencies that pull you back "in" the system. There is a better way.

You must transfer your coaching plan to your daily schedule. It is imperative to schedule time for proactive coaching conversations on a consistent basis. This time must be blocked and made a priority. It can't be treated as something that can be overridden by urgent activities that arise. Canceling QCC sessions is an indirect message to your team that they are not important enough to receive your time.

KEY CONCEPT

Effective coaches have a plan, and consistently execute against it.

2. Execute the Plan - Having a plan is critical but only represents half the equation. The second equally critical component is timely execution of that plan. The best-laid plans that are not acted upon don't produce results. Of course, you don't deliberately create plans to not act upon them, but for different reasons this is an area where you fall short. It is important to realize that people judge you by your actions and not your intentions. Having a desire to coach your team does not yield any benefits.

Often, poor execution results from distractions that pull you back "in" the system. Those with management experience are cognizant of these distractions; we've all faced them. Some managers just happen to be better than others when it comes to managing through them.

Distractions include: receiving unplanned phone calls, co-workers stopping by for an unannounced visit, responding to e-mails, dealing with administrative tasks, getting bogged down with internal processes, etc. The list is endless. Distractions have the potential to fill every hour of every day. For some, they do. For the best, they don't.

Responding to e-mail can become a full-time job if allowed. It is urgent and ongoing. However, you don't get paid based on how quickly you respond to administrative e-mail. While a response is required, it shouldn't override time on your calendar allocated to QCC. Level 2 and 3 Coaches understand their primary responsibility is to develop the members of their team to improve productivity. You get paid to deliver results. Activities that don't align with this responsibility should not get in the way of those that do. Dealing with nonessential management activities should be worked in around essential coaching activities. Not the other way around.

3. Minimize Upward Delegation – Many of you allow members of your team to delegate tasks up to you, a surefire way to reduce leverage and get sucked back "in" the system.

An individual incapable of executing part of a key process provides an excellent illustration of how upward delegation occurs. Assume an employee repeatedly has difficulty getting meetings scheduled with senior decision makers. However, her history shows that given the opportunity to get in front of these decision makers, she does an excellent job of establishing a strong consulting partnership. Her specific problem is breaking in and scheduling an appointment.

Rather than being coached to improve her strategy of engaging senior leaders, this individual looks to you to take this task off her plate. She knows you are good at this part of the process, and it is much quicker to have someone else perform this key activity for her. More importantly, you have a greater likelihood for success. Hard to blame the employee for going down this path!

What began as a status review meeting ends with you as the manager walking away with a to-do list that is longer than that of the employee. This is upward delegation.

Often you aren't consciously aware of this phenomenon, nor do you recognize your part in enabling this habit with your team. When people come to you with questions, you don't push back by utilizing QCC. Instead, you answer the question regardless of how ill-prepared your employee was for the conversation.

Answering questions with questions is an effective means for you to develop the critical thinking skills of your team while simultaneously reducing upward delegation. Your job is not to always provide answers.

Days are monopolized by people waiting to ask questions. A line, virtual or real, is formed at your desk. You may even complain about being constantly interrupted and not being able to accomplish personal goals because everyone is so dependent on you. Ironically, you fail to recognize your actions are the source of this employee behavior! By answering every question for your team, you create a vicious cycle where people are frozen by uncertainty and unable to perform their jobs on their own.

How do you respond when people come to you with questions? Do you answer them, or ask questions in return?

Let's take the example of a customer service representative seeking your opinion on how to deal with an upset customer and defuse a contentious situation. What would happen if you resisted the temptation to tell the employee what to do and instead turned the tables and asked the customer service rep for his thoughts and recommendations? Odds are favorable that the individual has good ideas, but simply lacks confidence and needs reinforcement.

We previously spoke about how difficult it is to break a bad habit without a plan. Something must be offered to fill the void. Albert Einstein stated it best when he said, "Insanity is doing the same thing over and over again and expecting different results." Breaking the cycle and reducing upward delegation requires a fresh approach by managers.

What expectations have you communicated to your team about how they prepare prior to coming to you with a question? If you have communicated expectations, do you enforce them or instead let people off the hook when they are not prepared? It is important to establish a repeatable process to ensure individuals are adequately prepared for meetings with you. Challenge them to think through the following questions before they engage you in a discussion:

KEY CONCEPT

Expectations When Seeking Assistance

What is the situation?

What are you trying to accomplish?

What actions do you recommend? Why?

What are the potential implications of these actions?

The short-term goal of this process is to transfer ownership of developing solutions from you to your employee. The long-term goal is to develop the confidence and critical thinking skills of your team, reduce their dependency on you, and minimize upward delegation. All of which improve your position of leverage.

For some members of your team, the response to this new process will be frustration. What used to be an easy conversation requiring little preparation now requires forethought. Activities that previously were taken on by you may come back into their lap. However, this frustration will be short-lived as employees begin to appreciate having the opportunity to develop their skills and become more effective and independent.

To illustrate the benefits of this process, we refer to a scenario in which a salesperson (SP) asks his sales manager (SM) to secure access into key accounts for him, as his efforts to date were unsuccessful. Let's review how the conversations might go using the traditional approach, and then compare this to how it might go utilizing our proposed process.

Scenario A (Traditional Approach)

SP: Hey boss, how are you? Thanks for your time.

SM: No problem, I'm looking forward to reviewing your pipeline. It looks like you have some exciting opportunities in your territory. Why don't we start with

Herbert Enterprises; how are things going?

SP: That would be a great place to start, as I could really use your help with this account. Their contract renewal is coming up in 6 months so we need to move quickly, as time is of the essence. Based on what we know, it should be a very good match for our product and service capabilities. It is definitely a place that we can compete on a level playing field with the incumbent vendor.

SM: I completely agree, plus, it represents a sizeable account in comparison to your current customer base. So where are we?

SP: I have spoken to several people in the organization and had decent conversations. First, I spoke to John Doe in the purchasing department to better understand what they are looking for in their Request for Proposal. I also spoke to Jane Doe, who is the executive assistant to the EVP of marketing, Jim Smith. I thought her personal insight into Jim might be helpful.

SM: Interesting. So have you spoken directly to Jim?

SP: No, I haven't. I left him a voicemail but he hasn't returned my call. That's alright though, because I think an indirect approach might be better in this situation. I'm going to continue to work through John and Jane. I think they will play a significant role in the decision-making process.

SM: So what do you need me to do with this account?

SP: Now that you ask, it would be great if you could make the call to Jim. That would really help me with all that I have going on right now. Plus, I don't always connect that well with senior executives like him.

SM: Alright, why don't you forward me Jim's contact info and I will try to connect with him. I'm really busy through Friday, but should have time early next week. I'll keep you posted.

SP: Great, I can't wait to hear about your conversation. Thanks!

Although a made-up scenario, similar conversations take place in organizations all the time. Although it takes different turns along the way, the final destination is often the same: a manager assuming responsibility to complete tasks for members of their team. There may be instances when this approach makes perfect sense, but often it doesn't and it is arrived at by happenstance. It is an employee pulling his boss back "in" the system to compensate for his shortcomings.

You should not take on the tasks of your team unless it is done in a strategic and purposeful manner. A Level 3 Coach assigns responsibilities to members of her team in a purposeful manner during coaching conversations. Doing otherwise allows you to get sucked back "in" the system.

Let's use the same situation to highlight how this conversation might sound when using the strategies of QCC and the previously outlined process.

Scenario B (QCC Approach)

SP: Hey boss, how are you? Thanks for your time.

SM: No problem, I'm looking forward to reviewing your pipeline. It looks like you have some exciting opportunities in your territory. Why don't we start with Herbert Enterprises; can you provide a quick update as to where we are in the sales process?

SP: I sure can. That would be a great place to start, as I could really use your help with that one. Their contract renewal is coming up in 6 months. As you know, it is a competitively held account and one that we have been trying to penetrate for some time. Based on what we know, it should be a very good match for our product and service capabilities. It is definitely a place that we can compete on a level playing field with the incumbent.

Original SM Response: I completely agree, plus, it represents a sizeable account in comparison to your current customer base. So where are we?

Not a poor or atypical response, but it didn't capitalize on the coaching opportunity presented in the opening dialogue. Additional clarification questions need to be asked to better understand the current situation; Step 1 in the Coaching Conversation Process. The conversation and associated questions could be:

Alternative SM Response: I agree this is a sizeable opportunity. You stated that our product and service capabilities "should be a good match for their organization." Can you elaborate on that? What do we know that led you to this conclusion? How did you determine this? What is the cost to us if we are incorrect in determining this?

Assuming this is a good opportunity, let's continue with the conversation.

SP: I have spoken to several people in the organization and had decent conversations. First, I spoke to John Doe in the purchasing department to better understand what they are looking for in their Request for Proposal. He was pretty open to answering my questions and the information he provided will be helpful as we shape our strategy. I also spoke to Jane Doe, who is the executive assistant to the EVP of marketing, Jim Smith. I thought her personal insight into Jim might be helpful. She gave some good insight into Jim's personality and style.

SM: Interesting. So have you spoken directly to Jim?

SP: No, I haven't. I left him a voicemail but he hasn't returned my call. That's alright though, because I think an indirect approach might be better in this situation. I am making good progress with John and Jane, and I think they will play a significant role in the decision-making process.

SM: So what do you need me to do with this account?

Alternative SM Response: Why do you think John and Jane will play a significant role in the decision-making process? How did you come to this conclusion? What is the risk of being wrong about this assumption? Would it be helpful if we spent some time developing a strategy to better understand the significance of their roles?

You mentioned you left Jim a voicemail, but he didn't return your call? Tell me what you said in your message. How do you feel you could adjust your message to increase the likelihood of him returning your call? What other strategies do you have to try and connect with him? What did you learn about his style from his assistant that might be helpful in developing this strategy?

It is impossible to 'script' a coaching conversation. Level 3 Coaches navigate through conversations by adjusting their line of questioning based on specific responses to previous questions. There are many branches on the conversation tree. Good coaches leverage the four strategic question categories to maximize impact.

The point of reviewing the above example is to demonstrate how you often take responses to questions at face value and don't probe further to clarify the situation. Even the most incompetent employee can learn how to answer cursory questions to your satisfaction. However, when challenged for more specifics, cracks begin to show around additional coaching opportunities.

Remember, people have unique strengths. Process constraints show up in different places for members of a team. People who prove over time they are proficient in certain areas don't require the depth of questions when coaching.

4. Define your Accessibility – You get sucked back "in" the system because you haven't defined how your team should access you when they need something. Often you make yourself available to every beck and call, constantly being pulled off task from interruptions.

The most precious resource you have is your time. Everyone operates on a level playing field when it comes to how many hours are in a day, but Level 2 and 3 Coaches are more effective in how they choose to invest this resource. That is why it is so important to create and execute a plan. The purpose of a plan is to ensure the right activities are consistently performed and time is maximized on essential activities that will create the greatest lift. Not establishing expectations for how your team should access you is an obstacle to this goal.

Yes, your role as a manager is to develop the talents of your team and generate measurable results. However, that doesn't mean that employees can interrupt you at their every whim!

Whether your employees are located in the next cubicle, a different city, or halfway across the country, interruptions are just a moment away. In the world of technology today, workers don't have to be in the same physical room with you for this to occur. E-mails, instant messaging, texting, voicemails, cell phones, desk phones, and social media tools all provide immediate access to you from your team. These virtual interruptions cause the same amount of chaos in a schedule as does someone walking into your office with a question.

Instead of allowing your team to hit you up every time a thought comes to mind for which they want your opinion or insight, have them write it down and accumulate a list of topics for your next formal one-on-one coaching session. This process does several things: it minimizes disruptions for you, forces employees to bundle and prioritize their questions; and, in some cases, completely eliminates items from making the list. Some items simply fall away because in the moment they seemed urgent, but their importance faded as they were framed up against other topics.

This only works if your team knows that they have dedicated time on your calendar. If you ask them to bundle ideas for future discussions, yet you don't provide a forum to accomplish this, people will revert back to whatever means it takes to get answers. You open the interruption floodgates! Conversely, with positive reinforcement, people will happily gather items for future discussions knowing that these opportunities will be afforded adequate time at a designated meeting.

Members of a team need to understand and appreciate the value of time — theirs and yours. A manager who is too accessible goes against this premise.

CLOSING THOUGHT

Working "on" the system is a critical success factor for Level 2 and 3 Coaches. You cannot afford to spend precious time working "in" the system performing activities for your team. Your job is to create leverage by developing the skills of your team and facilitating the development of solutions that moves the group forward.

It is critical that you create a plan to ensure time is invested in "on" system activities. Use your calendar as a tool to block one-on-one QCC time with members of your team. Don't allow your plan to be disrupted with urgent activities, including interruptions by your employees. To reduce upward delegation, set expectations with your employees to think through the following questions before coming to you for help:

- What is the situation?
- What are you trying to accomplish?
- What actions do you recommend? Why?
- What are the potential implications of these actions?

CALL TO ACTION

- ❑ Block off one hour per week for the next month. Devote this time to a critical "on" system activity that will improve the performance of your team. Limit your accessibility during this time; put your "out of office" response on and shut down your e-mail for the hour.
- ❑ Identify an employee that consistently interrupts you throughout the week. Schedule a recurring one-on-one discussion with this employee. In the initial meeting, set the expectation with him to not interrupt you when he has questions, but instead to compile a list of topics for review in your recurring meetings.
- ❑ In addition, provide your team with the four questions above and tell them they must come prepared with answers to these questions for any topic they wish to discuss.

SECTION 4

The Turbo-Charged Results

Chapter 12
Turbo-Charging Individual Performance

As we move into the fourth, and final, section, let's take a moment to review the key concepts previously introduced.

Section I introduced the Fundamentals of Coaching. Early chapters focused on the power and benefits of coaching, the differences between managing and coaching, and the importance of both. In addition, the core elements of QCC were introduced, including the Coaching Conversation Process, establishing a predictable coaching frequency, coaching to relevant topics, and reaching mutual agreement. The powerful concept of "on" versus "in" was introduced as a means to distinguish which activities you perform generate the greatest lift.

Section II focused on the Fundamentals of Questions. The Question Continuum© was introduced and emphasized the importance of establishing trust with employees when using questions. The Strategic Question Model provided a process to use questions in coaching sessions to diagnose problems, determine satisfaction levels of those being coached, and how to willingly get people to spring into action after coaching sessions.

Section III provided a methodology to execute the fundamentals outlined in the first two sections. A system was provided to identify where to coach, how to coach to employee strengths, and how to effectively work "on" the system to turbo-charge performance for you and your team.

Section IV describes the turbo-charged results you achieve by consistently performing these practices. This section helps you recognize how performance improves and leverage increases, both from an individual and team perspective. This chapter focuses on the turbo-charging of individual results stemming from QCC.

Leverage is one of the most important concepts in this book. Your success as a manager hinges on your ability to improve leverage by investing time in the right activities.

The demands you face today are significant. Tolerance for underperformers has grown increasingly short. Organizations are under significant stress resulting from eroding economic conditions. Aggressive goals will not be achieved by executing the same old strategy.

Time and expense do not allow you to correct mistakes made by struggling employees. You can no longer afford to put people on your shoulders and carry them across the finish line. Instead, you must create leverage by developing the knowledge, skills, and confidence of your team through QCC. Only by coaching others and asking the right questions at the right time will you accomplish this goal.

A command-and-control management style has its place, but those places are few and far between in today's organizations. The modern professional workforce is highly educated, well informed and very talented. The best employees not only have a desire to succeed, but they also thrive on being developed by their manager and growing professionally. Top performers gravitate toward leaders and coaches who can make them better. The best individual contributors are not interested in being told what to do. These professionals want to understand and be involved in the process. QCC addresses that need.

The concept of leverage was introduced in Chapter 1. Power and effectiveness are generated from leverage. With leverage you can more easily accomplish greater professional, economic, and political change. When QCC is properly applied, leverage manifests itself in the three ways listed below:

KEY CONCEPT

The Manifestation of Leverage

Turbo-Charging Individual Performance

1. People Producing Faster

2. Higher Engagement Levels

3. Increased Retention

The remainder of this chapter explores the three forms of leverage that turbo-charge individual performance, and Chapter 13 focuses on the three forms of leverage that turbo-charge team performance.

1. People Producing Faster

Unproductive employees cause a significant drag on the operating cost of any organization. The longer this time is extended, the greater the impact to the bottom line. QCC shortens the time it takes for individuals to become productive, accelerating their journey down the path to success.

Select industries are experiencing significant growth during this challenging economic cycle. Although growth is exciting, it adds stress and strain to an organization.

Oftentimes the rate at which new employees are brought into an organization exceeds the functional capacity of the managers. This happens in two ways: the organization physically doesn't have enough managers to effectively lead the larger employee base, or the manager population is not equipped to effectively coach others. Either way, the result is the same, lost opportunity due to a coaching capacity shortage.

A common indicator to gauge the long-term success for a new employee is how effectively they perform after a defined period of time, say 90 days. The length of time it takes for a person to reach effectiveness depends on the complexity of the environment. When individuals demonstrate a propensity to perform at an early stage of their employment, there is a higher probability they will achieve long-term success. If they struggle significantly after 90 days, the likelihood of long-term success is diminished. You benefit greatly when you focus on the early-term success of new employees.

Several factors lead to early success. First, did the selection process identify an individual that is a good fit for the position? Second, did the individual receive timely and effective training in the areas critical to his job? Lastly, and perhaps most importantly, did the individual receive adequate one-on-one coaching from his manager during this critical development period?

Too frequently the answer to these questions, especially the last one, is a resounding no. The organization indeed may have hired the individual with the best talent and fit for the position, but companies often drop the ball in terms of how effectively they formally bring people into the organization.

While this is not a book on interviewing, selecting, or hiring people, it is important you don't overlook a key element impacting the long-term fit of new employees: the culture of the organization, department or team. Cultures are not interchangeable, and the ability of a new employee to integrate into a new culture is underappreciated.

Understanding the culture of the organization from which the new hire comes from, combined with the experience he has upon joining your organization, provides critical insight for how to train and coach a new employee.

Investing in training is an oxymoron in many organizations. Companies see it as a necessary evil and shortcuts are pursued by senior leaders to get new employees productive as soon as possible. Proper training is important for more than obvious reasons.

New employees need a thorough understanding of what it is they support. But beyond products or services, your team's processes (how you do stuff) is learned during training sessions. You begin to set expectations as to how the employee will perform via how processes are completed. The importance of response time, attention to detail, efficiency, or lack thereof, are all initially communicated during training sessions.

A Personal Experience – Lack of Cultural Awareness

For a span of five years I worked as an independent consultant with public and private firms spanning dozens of industries. One client was a statewide network of offices that directly served consumers. Turnover plagued the receptionist position. While investigating causes of this recurring problem it became apparent why; new hires were thrust into their role with little formal training. At most, they were shown how to check in clients via their computer and what paperwork was required. However, they weren't equipped with knowledge about the broader culture and operating expectations. No one provided guidance on how to handle situations in which the phone is ringing and a client is at the counter, what the client wait time expectations were, and why specific paperwork had to be filled out.

The new receptionists were trained on the bare bones procedural elements of the job, yet that only scratched the surface in terms of positioning them to be successful. Cultural expectations were not communicated. Zero coaching was provided. This compounded in making it a very stressful position that experienced unacceptable turnover.

Think of the impact this had on their bottom line. Not just the turnover, but the losses of repeat client revenue. The receptionist was the first contact the client had when walking in or calling for an appointment. He or she was literally the face of the organization.

After this problem was identified, the organization took steps to formally onboard new receptionists. Turnover decreased. In fact, upon a recent visit to one of their offices I was greeted by a familiar face; one of the receptionists whom I worked with over fifteen years ago!

Another overlooked benefit of training is the development of employee confidence. Good training creates confidence in people by establishing expectations for them in their role. Proper training allows employees to focus and concentrate on uncovering and satisfying customer needs and delivering value to both clients and the company.

The cumulative effect of this training leads to employees learning and adding to the culture of your organization. One of the biggest reasons new employees fail to acclimate is their lack of ability or sensitivity to understand and engage around the culture of the new organization. New employees with experience at other organizations often refer to "how I did it at my other employer." Clearly, there are learning and best practice opportunities for the employee's new company; however, we have found a direct success connection to the new employee's ability to rapidly adapt to the new culture.

Okay, so you hired the right person. You provided quality training around their key responsibilities. Everything is great, right? Well, maybe. Did you perform regularly scheduled coaching sessions with the new trainee? Did you use QCC to reinforce the culture and expectations with your new team member?

You made a very large investment by bringing on a new person to your team. QCC allows you to maximize that investment. QCC also allows you to evaluate the performance of your newest team member. Does she understand the products or services your company offers? Is she learning the key processes associated with her role? Is she fitting in with your culture? Is she gaining confidence? Coaching answers these questions and simultaneously reinforces key messages.

For most organizations, the best-case scenario when developing new employees is that they receive timely and effective product, service, and process training. This is a noble effort, but, surprisingly enough, even this is not provided by all companies today. Even if thorough training is part of the on-boarding process, it is simply not enough. Training and coaching are two different disciplines. Coaching must accompany and complement training.

Training focuses on the acquisition of knowledge, and coaching focuses on the application of knowledge. They are closely linked. New employees who receive classroom training must be coached to effectively retain and apply this knowledge on a go-forward basis.

Without knowing how to apply knowledge, the likelihood of a new employee being successful is greatly diminished. QCC improves the application and relevancy of knowledge and leads to long-term employee success.

Level 2 and 3 Coaches tailor QCC to the specific needs and talents of the individual receiving the coaching. Every individual is unique, and it is unrealistic to think that a generic coaching approach can be applied to all members of a team. People learn in different ways, bring different experiences to bear in their role, and are motivated for different reasons. A job title doesn't define a position as much as the unique talents that the person filling the role does.

An effective coach spends time early on with a new team member gaining insight into what makes her tick. As former college football coach Lou Holtz stated: "It's not my job to motivate players. They bring extraordinary motivation to our program. It's my job not to de-motivate them." The same principle is applied to the world of coaching.

Executing a defined coaching strategy during the first 90 days is critical to the short- and long-term success of your new team member. If you don't have the capacity to dedicate formal one-on-one coaching time to a new employee, don't hire them.

Too often we assume people can be successful on their own.

Research shows that an employee is never more engaged than during the first six months of her employment. Therefore, this is a crucial time for effective coaching to take place. People left fending for themselves during this important stage of development will take longer to become productive members of the team. QCC accelerates the time it takes for new employees to be productive.

2. Higher Engagement Levels

A second way leverage manifests itself is through higher employee engagement levels. The Gallup Organization conducts extensive research regarding the subject of Employee Engagement®. Not only is the work interesting, it is extremely relevant.

Gallup calculates Employee Engagement by measuring the intensity of employee responses to twelve specific questions, referred to as the Q12. The results of the Q12 provide a measure of engaged employees to disengaged employees, and more importantly, a correlation to employee productivity, retention, profitability, and customer satisfaction. As Employee Engagement improves, so do these resulting measures.

Why is this relevant in a book about coaching? Well, like other research, Gallup identifies the quality of the manager as a key lever driving employee engagement. A new team member must understand his strengths and secure a role that is a good fit for those strengths, but most importantly he must work for the right manager.

This points back to the old adage that still rings true today: people don't quit a company, they quit their manager. Maybe you have worked for a manager whose actions caused you to be disengaged; they took credit for the success of others, pointed the finger when there were failures, or spent their time working "in" the system. This path does not create an empowered, high-performing team.

Ultimately, you want to grow and continue to be challenged by your manager. Your engagement level wanes if you don't have a solid and productive relationship with your manager; this is true for both high and low performers.

So how do you know if your employees are engaged? Sometimes it is obvious based on performance and behavior, but not always. Below is the same Two-Step

Closed Loop Model we introduced earlier in the book:

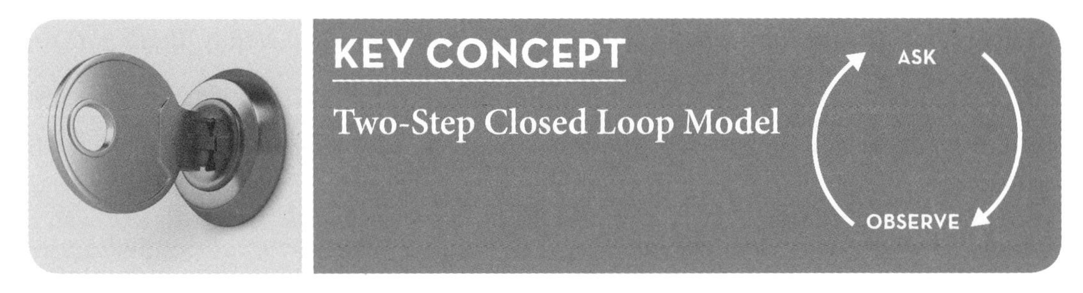

The model is very simple. Ask effective questions of your team and then take time to observe their behavior, activities, and results. Evaluate whether your observations align with the answers to your questions. This simple formula is an outstanding "Early Warning System" and creates a basis to address opportunities or issues before they become problematic. Below are two examples:

Example 1

Coach: *Beth, you sounded really excited on today's conference call. Your results from last month are ahead of plan. You must feel great about that!*

Beth: *I really do. The plan I put in place after our last one-on-one meeting really helped me. I guess I knew all along I needed to do that, but in answering your questions it became obvious I needed to get on that right away. I did it, and the results are showing.*

Coach: *That's outstanding, Beth. We have a new team member in the Chicago office that could benefit from a similar solution. How would you feel about sharing your success and what you've learned with him? Can you think of some important questions to ask him about his situation?*

Beth: *You bet; I would love to do that. I bet he could really benefit from what I learned.*

Let's review what the coach learned from this brief conversation. The coach,

- Confirmed Beth is engaged.
- Learned that Beth appreciated and benefited from coaching.
- Further motivated Beth by encouraging her to share her success story and help another person on the team by leveraging the principles of QCC.

Example 2

Coach: *Jim, good to see you. How are you doing?*

Jim: *Great. Everything is going pretty well.*

Coach: *I noticed you were quiet in last week's off-site planning meeting. That's not "the Jim" I'm used to.*

Jim: *It's no big deal. I just ran into a few issues with our operations area. It will probably work out.*

Coach: *So what's up with operations?*

Jim: *Operations is telling me our new product launch could be delayed six months. I've pre-sold this to eight clients. If we can't meet our dates, the company and I will lose credibility, not to mention my commission.*

What can be learned if the conversation stops here?

- Jim, a solid performer, isn't so happy after all.
- We have a problem in operations.
- Jim feels his credibility is on the line.
- Jim is worried about his income.

These are really big engagement issues. By knowing about them now, you can deal with them before they become bigger issues. It is important to note that you learned all of this after Jim said everything was "great" and "going pretty well."

You may have employees that don't want to rock the boat or be seen as complainers, or they just feel compelled to work things out themselves. By asking effective diagnostic questions followed by observation, you are able to uncover and manage critical issues before your team experiences declining engagement levels. This prevents an all-too-common scenario where people quit their jobs but forget to tell their managers! They keep showing up for work every day but make minimal impact.

3. Improved Retention

What would the impact be to your bottom line if you could retain a greater percentage of your team? Few organizations do a good job of calculating the cost of turnover. Poor retention leads to higher organization costs in the following ways:

- Loss of invested training time and dollars with the departing employee.
- Lost business while the position goes unoccupied.
- Lost business from customers who chose to take their business with the departing employee.
- Cost to post or advertise the open position(s).

- Cost for executive search firms, or time spent at job fairs recruiting.
- Time and cost to screen and interview candidate(s).
- Potential signing bonus for the new employee.
- Cost to train the new employee.
- Time to get the new employee productive.

After reviewing this list, and doing some mental math, the staggering cost of poor employee retention is easy to see. Ask your Human Resources department about the cost of turnover and they will quickly tell you it's between one and one and a half times the salary of the people you are replacing!

QCC creates increased confidence and skill for a team member, leading to increased levels of key activities, productivity, and higher retention. Success breeds success, and there is no getting around this simple yet powerful model. It is hard to argue that people achieving goals and receiving positive recognition are less likely to leave an organization than those that aren't.

QCC emphasizes six steps in the Retention Model shown below.

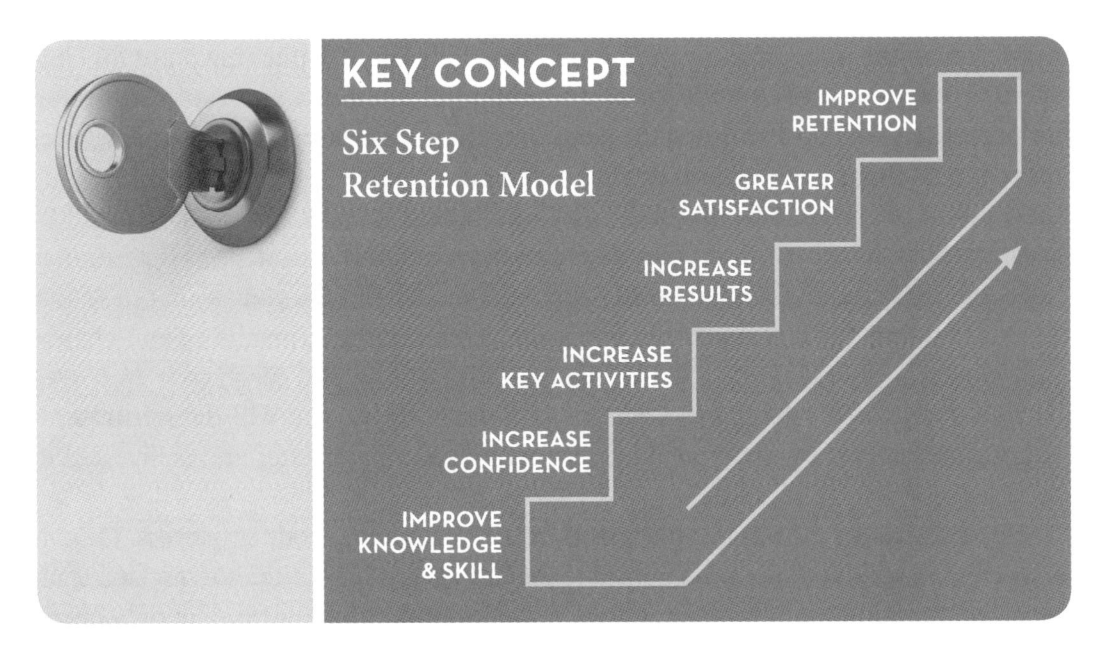

The first step to increase retention on your team is to improve the knowledge and skill of your team. QCC increases the speed and effectiveness that employees are able to perform in their role and sustains this higher level of performance over time.

As an employee's knowledge and skills improve, so does her confidence. There is a direct link. Confidence is a subjective, emotional state of mind achieved when a chosen course of action is known to be the best or most effective given the circumstances. Once employees understand the intricacies of their job, their core responsibilities, and what expectations you have of them, their confidence level soars. They feel better about their ability to accomplish objectives. Enthusiasm increases and becomes noticeable to others.

As confidence increases, employees eagerly approach the key activities associated with their job; activities that, if focused on, lead to superior results. Team members who aggressively focus on these key activities produce better results than those that don't.

Team members experience greater satisfaction by meeting stated goals, achieving a greater sense of accomplishment and professionalism. People enjoy doing things at which they excel. It becomes its own closed-loop motivational model. Enthusiasm becomes contagious.

Not surprisingly, the more someone enjoys her job, the more likely she is to stick around, resulting in improved retention.

Evaluate yourself and your team against the Steps to Retention. If you need direction on where or what to coach members of your team, the Steps to Retention model points you in the right direction. The model provides a good launching point for conversations and becomes a basis for asking insightful questions. It is not uncommon for people to move up and down the steps over the course of their employment. Factors contributing to this up and down movement on the Steps to Retention include the amount of change affecting their position, taking on new core duties, a shift in organizational focus, etc. Assessing where employees fall on the Steps to Retention is not a one-time exercise. Continuously apply the model and ask your team questions. Are you finding that a particular individual has hit a slump? There is a good chance they moved backward on the "Steps." Dig in, ask questions, and coach your employee back to success. By taking these actions and using QCC, you will demonstrate to your team that you are the type of leader that makes others better and is invested in their success

There are numerous benefits that result from you coaching your employees. QCC is a concrete method for you to demonstrate interest and caring for the success of a team member. At a minimum, everyone appreciates an investment of time from his or her boss.

Consciously or unconsciously, how you spend your time is a good indicator of what ranks high on your priority list. People conclude they are important and relevant if you spend one-on-one time with them. This includes high performers. Don't assume your top employees are not interested in being coached. By ignoring them, you send the unintended message that they are not that important, eroding their engagement levels and creating a much higher retention risk. Top performers can and should receive coaching.

Beyond the obvious investment of time, an effective QCC session is the most productive means for you to build the talents, skills, and knowledge of an employee. Too often you assume employees are more capable than they truly are. This inaccurate assumption causes you to spend too little time focused on developing the specific skills of your employees. Often, the end result is an employee with a big goal who is not prepared, setting them up to be a potential retention risk. It is a vicious cycle — one that cannot be broken without a deliberate and effective plan.

CLOSING THOUGHT

QCC compresses the ramp-up time for new employees to become productive. Leaving individuals to fend for their own development without the benefit of coaching is a risky proposition. Before hiring a new employee, first confirm that you have the capacity to invest time with him on his development. Sending someone to training is a great strategy, but without reinforcement and follow-up it has diminished long-term value. Training is not a substitute for coaching. They are both important and interdependent. Effective coaching leads to higher engagement levels and increased retention.

CALL TO ACTION

- ❑ Define and communicate expected results for new employees for their first 18 months on the team. Establish 90-day, 6-month, 12-month and 18-month goals. Evaluate progress against goals and monitor momentum.
- ❑ Explain the culture of the organization. Use examples to illustrate points.
- ❑ Outline the training curriculum for the new hire. Confirm expectations.
- ❑ Develop coaching strategies to overlay and complement existing training programs. Immediately apply QCC principles to individuals who complete formal training, with the focus on how this new knowledge applies to their process.
- ❑ Introduce the "Steps to Success" model and ask employees what step they feel they are on.
- ❑ Evaluate employees against the "Steps" model and identify coaching opportunities.

Chapter 13

Turbo-Charging Team Performance

Chapter 12 focused on the turbo-charger effect that QCC has on individual performance. Three ways in which leverage manifests itself at this level were introduced. The first element highlighted how new employees or people in new positions can accelerate their path to productivity. It was emphasized how the right combination of culture, training, and reinforcement through QCC turbo-charges early productivity and creates more rapid success.

The second element provided insight into getting the best people have to offer through higher engagement levels. Not surprisingly, people who are into their jobs and careers and feel a connection to the team around them outperform those that don't. QCC reinforces and supports employee engagement. Asking the right questions, listening to the responses, and observing behavior creates a high-performing team.

Improving the retention of high-performing managers or employees turbo-charges an organization like few other productivity tools. The Steps to Retention model highlighted the progression level employees experience through QCC. This provides you with an excellent tool to diagnose where to coach individual members of your team.

KEY CONCEPT

The Manifestation of Leverage

Turbo-Charging Team Performance

1. Increased Productivity

2. Greater System Insight

3. Lower Management Expense

1. Increased Productivity

Various research sources show a correlation between effective coaching and business results. One such study from a large multinational research organization focuses on the benefits of sales coaching. Their research reveals the number-one lever for developing confidence and achieving success for a salesperson is the quality of their manager. Surprisingly, this outranks other key categories such as sales skills training, compensation and rewards, development programs, and many other categories.

If you manage salespeople, you might be surprised to learn that training is not ranked first in terms of attributes that invoke a team member's confidence. Isn't training critical? The answer is yes, it is critical, both for new people to learn fundamental sales skills, and for skilled veterans to sharpen their saws. However, many organizations send people to training without having a defined plan to reinforce those skills through ongoing coaching upon their return to the job.

Research shows that without systematic coaching and follow-up, individuals lose significant portions of their training knowledge within thirty days. However, training combined with systematic coaching improves retention four-fold over training alone.

Too often you send employees to training and assume your work is complete. Upon the employees' return, you may ask if the training was beneficial and what they learned, but the greatest lift is achieved when you ask questions around how this new knowledge can be applied. Training is simply the first step in a series of activities that needs to occur to maximize production.

Digging deeper into the research shows the number-one attribute of the best managers is their ability to coach employees. Effective coaching that is executed on a consistent basis drives productivity. For example, in the sales environment, research shows teams receiving less than two hours of coaching per month underperform against their goal by an average of 10%. On average, teams that report receiving more than three hours of coaching per month exceed their goals by more than 7%.

Understanding what employees need the most is only half of the equation. What about the skills you possess; and more importantly, how those skills align with the needs of your team?

Ironically, research shows coaching is the number-one category or skill set that managers are least equipped to deliver. So what employees want the most, managers are ill-equipped to provide. Not exactly a recipe for success, and a primary reason for writing this book.

Before hiring or promoting a new leader, ask yourself questions about the most important needs of the team, and then hire a leader that aligns to those needs.

This key concept sounds simple and straightforward. Unfortunately, it is frequently ignored. Hiring managers revert back to "who is next in line," "who has the most impressive resume," or "who is the top-performing employee to be the next manager."

KEY CONCEPT

A Manager's Skills must be aligned to Team Members' Needs

An alternative approach will pay significant dividends. When selecting a new manager, first consider the needs and strengths of the team that is to be led. Select a manager that best aligns or fits with these needs and strengths to increase the likelihood of success and retention.

It's not unusual to have more than one highly qualified candidate to fill an open manager position. In determining the best candidate, consider selecting the individual that is the "best fit" for the job at hand. Do this by asking yourself or the hiring team questions about the immediate needs of the team to be led.

Examples of questions to consider include:

- How is the current team performing?
- Are they exceeding goals or in need of immediate help?
- How experienced is the team?
- What are the three things, that if done exceptionally well, will take the team to the next level?
- How will the industry / environment change over the next year, and what impact will that have on the team?
- What are the key development needs of the team?
- What type of leadership style will drive the best results from today's team?
- Are the people that would surround a new leader (peers and direct reports) experienced or novices in their roles?

Answering these and similar questions will go a long way to pointing you in the right direction for hiring your next leader. Aligning the needs of the team to the skills of the new leader will turbo-charge results much more than simply promoting the "next person in line."

As referenced in earlier chapters, in order for coaching to be effective, it must be customized and specific to each individual being coached. This same principle can be applied at a higher level; each team and organization is unique, and your coaching models must be flexible to accommodate these differences. When this is done, productivity increases.

2. Greater System Insight

System Insight is the in-depth knowledge about the people and processes for which you are responsible. The ability to lead a high-performance organization increases significantly when you are able to harness this powerful knowledge. Without it, you coach your team with one arm tied behind your back.

Let's assume you have worked for your current employer for many years. You understand the business model and how it has evolved over time. You know the culture, people, competitive advantages and disadvantages, and the key processes that allow the organization to function. This is a System Insight. QCC turbo-charges your ability to transfer this System Insight to others in the organization.

System Insight isn't obtained by skimming the surface utilizing traditional management techniques. Only so much knowledge can be acquired by reviewing reports and holding weekly team calls. The best means to reach this profound level of understanding is by leveraging QCC; only then can you go beneath the surface and truly understand the situation at hand.

Developing the capabilities of your team is one of your primary responsibilities as a leader. This requires the use of effective questions to uncover needs and develop specific coaching plans for each person; plans that are inclusive of their unique talents, skills, and knowledge. The goal of a manager is to determine the best means to leverage these talents and put each individual in a position to succeed as frequently as possible.

Many of you reading this book are likely parents. The area of gaining greater system insight easily translates from organizations to your home.

The role of a parent is to understand the unique talents, skills, and knowledge of his or her children, and coach them to success. Doing this requires a deep understanding of the challenges they face, how their skills align with their classwork and extra-curricular activities, and identifying the types of scenarios which provide them with the greatest opportunity for success. This insight can't be obtained without the use of questions.

It doesn't take a parenting guru to realize that kids don't always respond favorably to being told what to do, especially as they grow older. There are negative consequences when a teenager is pushed too hard by a parent. The conversations are very one-sided, with the parent doing 95% of the talking; often the teenager is simply along for the ride. What little common ground existed before the discussion is likely out the window at its conclusion. The two sides are further apart than they were to begin with.

More importantly, this approach does not provide the parents with any deep insight as to what the source of the problems may be. They know nothing more about why this is happening, or how the problematic behavior can be changed. The only thing they know for sure is that they conveyed their message in an extremely direct manner. The parents may feel better, but the problem is unlikely to go away.

Conversely, using questions with children is an extremely effective means to gain valuable insight as to how one can become a better parent, creating opportunities to coach them through challenging situations. A few key questions can provide tremendous insight beyond what is displayed on the most recent report card. Report cards indeed provide a measured evaluation of their progress, but it would be inaccurate to assume that this single piece of information tells all that one needs to know.

What else is there? Potentially their grades are progressively getting worse, and the current grade doesn't reflect that trend. Maybe a poor grade in one class is eroding their confidence in others. It could be that they are investing huge amounts of time to complete the homework for one class at the sacrifice of all the others. From the surface, everything appears to be in order, but issues lurk in the depths below.

It is not sufficient to simply ask a child how school was today. A generic question will yield a generic answer; "fine" will be the likely response. Not much system insight obtained there! If parents left it at that, the potential of facing a serious problem at the end of the semester goes up exponentially.

To obtain deep system insight requires additional questions that stimulate open and honest dialogue. Examples could include the following:

- I see you had a B on a math test; is this grade what you were expecting to receive?
- How do your homework grades compare to your quiz and test grades?
- Why do you think there is a difference?
- What types of things are you currently learning?
- What are the challenges you have with this concept?
- What would make you feel better prepared going into the next test?
- How can we improve this situation?

The list could go on and on, as there are many appropriate questions that would generate good dialogue. The critical point is that the responses to these questions give the parent an enormous amount of system insight. This insight goes well beyond what is stated on the report card. Insight that otherwise would remain buried is now available, and it is extremely valuable and applicable when formulating the plan to improve performance.

The same principles about asking effective questions to gain system insight apply to conversations with your employees. Asking questions that elicit surface responses will not provide insight into the true situation, nor will this allow you to create an effective coaching plan.

The process model introduced in chapter 5 talked about the importance of coaching to the input side of the process. It is impossible to manage what has already occurred. You need to shift from managing outputs to coaching inputs. This requires conversations, not reports, and is true at home or when working with a team at work. In fact, the best way to improve outputs is to spend more time on inputs.

KEY CONCEPT

Coach inputs and don't manage outputs

The information age has ushered in an entirely new era in terms of reporting capabilities for many organizations. You no longer run 'blind' when it comes to monitoring the performance results for your team. At the click of a mouse you can review the performance of an individual or the collective roll-up for an entire division. You likely have abundant performance metrics at your fingertips.

You must avoid the temptation to operate in a command-and-control mode, spending more time in your office reviewing numbers, instead of spending time observing and assessing the specific capabilities of your team. You can't assume reports tell the whole story.

A brief conversation with a team member is often more eye-opening than any report. There is tremendous value in the reports, and it is important you prepare for coaching conversations by reviewing the latest data. There is no substitute for QCC and the accompanying insight that comes with it. QCC allows you to learn about the important details affecting the performance of your team, as well as identifying future coaching opportunities. QCC focuses on the input side of the process with the goal of driving greater results.

System insight can't be garnered by your sitting behind a desk. It requires planned and purposeful time with each team member, both observing and demonstrating the desired activities.

3 - Lower Management Expense

The leverage generated via QCC accrues not only to the benefit of the engaged individuals, but it also manifests itself in the form of lower management expense. As leverage increases, time expands.

KEY CONCEPT

As leverage increases, time expands

If new team members produce faster, they require less "training" time. If your team is more engaged, turnover goes down. You spend less time looking for replacements.

As you get better at QCC, your team becomes more effective. This improved effectiveness leads to increased efficiency as your time can now be invested in activities that generate sustainable results. This approach is much different than being absorbed in repetitive routines such as revolving door hiring and recurring discussions with poor performers on your team that chew up precious time.

The net result of the leverage can be translated into broader spans of control and even fewer layers of management. If you have to spend excessive time recruiting, training, and "managing out" poor performers, you will never get ahead. There just isn't enough remaining time to spend coaching good performers. For example, if organizations can reduce the time managers work "in" the system, or improve retention rates, fewer managers are needed. Productivity and revenue per full-time equivalent (FTE) goes up, and management expense is reduced.

A Personal Experience – Increased Management Expenses

We observed a common situation when working with a business that had retail stores located across the country. In this organization, regional managers had responsibility for a number of geographically distributed retail stores. Each outlet or location had a site manager and five to eight staff.

In this particular scenario, the regional manager loved to train people. Her typical mode of operation was to visit each store in her geography for several days each month. She would come to the store, bypass the store manager and conduct one-on-one training sessions with each salesperson in the office. It was very rewarding for her as she was able to connect with employees and always walked away knowing they were better as a result of her training.

It was very apparent to us that the regional manager was working "in" the system, performing the duties in place of the site manager. It was a classic example of a leader eroding the power and authority of a manager that works for them. Rather than coaching the site manager on how to be more effective in her role, the regional manager completely ignored them. If the salespeople in this office had a problem, they would go to the regional manager instead of their office manager. Instead of coaching the seven store managers in her region, she took on the management responsibility for each of the approximately 45 employees.

In our work with this client we showed the regional manager how to better leverage herself, improve results, and lower management expenses by coaching the seven store managers. She equipped her managers to deliver the same messages, training, and coaching that she previously delivered directly to the 45 salespeople.

She soon went from having seven disengaged managers to seven very engaged store managers. This allowed her to invest her time in other "on" system activities – activities that improved the environment for the entire region.

Results improved and everyone won. The sales results for the region were among the top in the country. Turnover went down because the store managers became Level 2 Coaches and could effectively develop each member of their team. It was much easier for the store managers to coach five to seven employees in the same office than it was for the regional manager to coach 45 people across multiple offices. The pipeline quality for future regional managers improved as the store managers gained new skills and experiences that were critical for them to move up in the organization. They applied new knowledge more effectively as a result of the questions they were asked by the regional manager in coaching conversations.

CLOSING THOUGHT

QCC turbo-charges manager leverage and leads to improved team performance. In addition to the humanistic benefits of leverage, QCC also drives improvements in efficiency. Quality QCC leads to increased productivity, greater system insight, and lower management expense.

CALL TO ACTION

- ❑ Review key data and reports as you prepare for your next coaching session. Based on the data, evaluate the needs of the overall team and the specific needs of each individual. Write down the questions around the data prior to your next coaching conversation process.
- ❑ Identify key areas where you lack the appropriate level of System Insight. Specify the activities you need to engage in to improve your insight in the systems that you manage. What types of questions can you ask your team to improve your insight in this area? When can you schedule time to observe one of your team members to evaluate his performance in this area while simultaneously expanding your knowledge?
- ❑ As you improve your coaching, identify a specific efficiency benefit that will accrue to your team or organization. Develop a way to measure this indicator to monitor the impact of your QCC.

Chapter 14
Taking Action

By reading this book, you now possess the knowledge to apply the principles of QCC within your team and organization. By putting these principles to work, you will in turn help your team members develop their knowledge, skills, and confidence, making them more independent and higher performing. The result of these collective efforts will improve the overall performance for you and your team.

This increased independence of your team results in additional time that you can use to work "on" the system, directing your attention to important activities that drive further productivity gains. That is leverage at its finest. To be successful in this endeavor, you must minimize distractions from less important activities that are urgent and unplanned.

Implementing this approach sounds simple and easy, but change is hard and behavioral habits are deeply etched in our subconscious mind. As humans, we are creatures of habit and we are most comfortable doing things that we have always done. For example, you likely get up at the same time every morning and perform a consistent routine as you get ready for the day. You drive the same route to work, get a cup of coffee at the same shop, park in the same section of the parking lot, begin your time in the office by reviewing e-mails and voicemail messages, and have lunch with the same co-workers. You stick to a regimented set of subconscious habits that, if not recognized, have the potential to diminish your effectiveness as a leader.

Your subconscious mind acts as a supercomputer and operates hundreds of times faster than your conscious mind, often doing things on auto-pilot without being aware. Think about a time when you drove to a familiar destination, only to arrive with little recollection of the journey it took to get there. That is an example of your subconscious mind at work.

When we are born, our brains and nervous systems are alive, but by the time we become adults we are less aware and more habit-bound. While the human brain has the capacity to dream big, be inquisitive, and build meaningful relationships with others, it is hardwired to do the opposite, making it difficult to break out of routines.

QCC necessitates you change your daily and weekly habits, requiring you to be more proactive in dedicating time to coach your team while simultaneously asking questions instead of providing answers to employee inquiries. Rather than behaving in a stimulus-response mode where you immediately react to things brought to your attention, QCC is predicated on taking a deliberate pause between the stimulus and response, choosing a different and more effective path.

It is unrealistic to think that you can instantly flip the switch and be highly skilled in the area of QCC. It will take time, practice, and self-reflection. Because of this, it is important to establish realistic expectations and personal goals around your efforts. You must be deliberate in planning, conducting, and reviewing your coaching sessions. Prior to a QCC conversation, think about how you will set the climate to build trust and determine what questions you will ask to engage the other person in meaningful dialogue. Conduct a post-conversation assessment to determine if your preparation was beneficial and whether the overall QCC session was effective. Don't abandon the process just because some sessions are less than perfect; rather, learn from reflection and adjust the process to refine what works best for you.

Similarly, set realistic expectations about how much time you can dedicate to coaching members of your team. Don't fool yourself into believing that next week you will spend twice as much time with every member of your team. This will only set you up for failure. There are many demands on your time, and it will take a concerted effort to evaluate what activities you can stop performing so that you can invest more time in coaching. Failing to achieve an unrealistic goal can be self-defeating and cause you to lose momentum with your efforts.

The first step in your journey requires you to stop working "in" the system and performing the work of your team. Elevate your vantage point and gradually shift your time to working "on" the system. Evaluate the activities that you perform today and determine which are not vital and yield minimal impact. It becomes a matter of choice.

It is important to recognize that not everyone on your team requires the same level of coaching. Tenure, knowledge, skill, and willingness to perform the key activities of the job all play a factor as to which employees will benefit the greatest from your coaching. Individual needs constantly change, and your job is to understand these changes and adjust your coaching plan accordingly.

Use the chart below to quantify where the greatest coaching opportunities exist on your team. The x-axis represents the willingness of the employee to perform the key activities of the role. The y-axis represents the capability of the employee to perform the key activities of the role. Place a dot for each employee on the chart based on the intersection of these two variables. The chart is divided into four quadrants which are defined below:

1. Not Capable but Willing – The lower right quadrant represents employees who are not capable of performing the key activities of the role, but who are very willing to do so and have significant upside potential. These individuals bring tremendous enthusiasm, positivity, and talent to the team, yet they lack the system insight and unique experiences associated with the job for which they have been hired. Employees in this box desire to be successful, are coachable, and have significant performance improvement potential; they represent the greatest opportunity on the team for improvement via QCC.

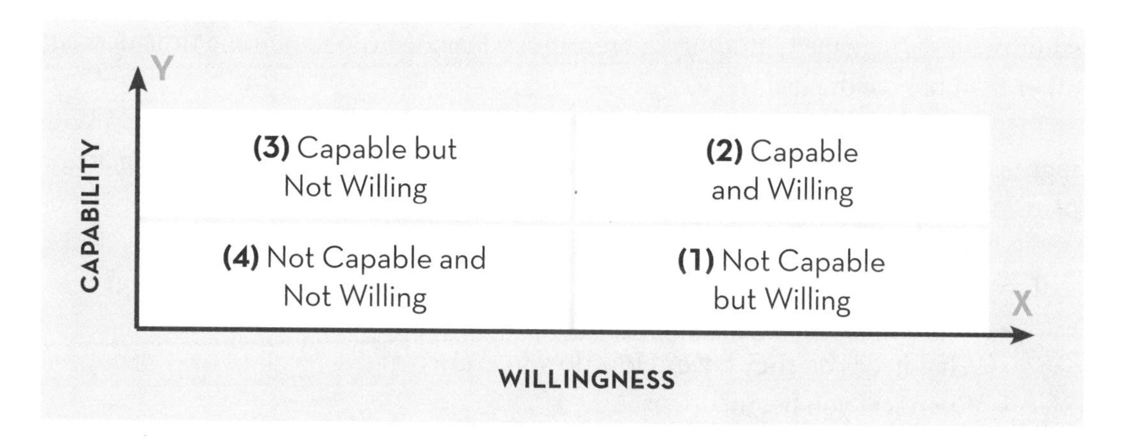

2. Capable and Willing – The upper right quadrant represents employees who are capable and willing to perform the key activities of the role. They are the top performers on the team and consistently deliver strong results. They bring enthusiasm, positivity, and talent to the role and also possess the system insight and unique experiences necessary to be successful. Employees in this box have performance improvement potential, albeit less than those in quadrant 1, and they often desire continued attention and coaching from their manager. Ignoring top performers from a coaching and recognition perspective can potentially decrease their engagement levels and make them a retention risk.

3. Capable but Not Willing – The upper left quadrant represents employees who are capable of performing the key activities of the role, but are not willing to do so. They have the capability to deliver strong results, yet for some reason they are choosing otherwise. These individuals possess the talent, system insight, and experience necessary to be successful, but they don't leverage these attributes to their potential. Employees in this box represent a coaching challenge that needs to be addressed through strong performance management. If left alone and allowed to continue with their ways, these employees will undermine the collective performance of the team.

4. Not Capable and Not Willing – The bottom left quadrant represents employees who are NOT capable of performing the key activities of the role and are NOT willing to learn. They are a poor fit for the team and potentially need to be managed out. Before you invest coaching time with these individuals, clear expectations must be set and closely managed. Without near-term improvement in their willingness to improve, along with measured progress against the stated performance goals, action must be taken to remove them from the team. Employees in this quadrant often consume precious management time and resources, leaving little remaining time to coach other members of the team.

Reflect and evaluate your team and plot each employee on the Capability / Willingness chart. Understanding the individual needs, develop a 60-day coaching action plan. When developing this plan consider the following questions:

1. Which member(s) of your team will you initially invest time in coaching?
    - Why them?
    - What needs do they have? How do you know?
    - When will you begin?

2. What specific actions will you take this week to initiate this plan?

3. What potential obstacles may arise that will make it difficult to follow through with your coaching action plan?

4. How can you plan for and overcome these obstacles?

5. Who will hold you accountable to your coaching action plan?
    - Why do you think this person will be effective in holding you accountable?
    - How will this be done?

6. What else do you need to do to ensure successful execution of your coaching action plan?

Identifying an individual to hold you accountable to your plan is critical. Share the details of your plan with a peer, manager, or coach. Ask her to meet with you and explain your goals, what action you have taken to date, how your coaching conversations are going, and what needs to be adjusted going forward. Having an accountability partner significantly improves your probability for success.

CLOSING THOUGHT

Our goal in writing this book was to provide others with the knowledge and process to become an effective Level 3 Coach. By achieving this status, you will realize improved individual and team performance. We concluded each chapter with brief "Closing Thoughts" and "Call to Actions." We recommend that these summaries be used as references as you implement QCC within your team and need quick reminders about key concepts.

There has never been a more important time to engage the hearts and minds of your team. The current economic climate requires that organizations perform at peak efficiency and effectiveness and harness the unique talents of each individual employee. The secret to unlocking this potential lies within your ability to effectively develop the critical thinking skills of your employees through QCC.

Enjoy and good luck!

Author biographies

Chick Herbert

Chick Herbert has twenty-five years of experience working in the public and private sectors as a senior business leader, speaker and executive coach. His successful career spans more than a dozen industries and provides Chick a wealth of experiential knowledge and perspective.

Chick has held senior leadership roles in organizational development, training, sales, human resources, marketing and operations. He currently is Vice President of Customer Excellence for Wells Fargo Retail Services. Previously Chick served as Vice President of Leadership Development and Talent Planning for Wells Fargo & Company and began his Wells Fargo career as Vice President of Global Sales Development for Wells Fargo Financial. Prior to joining Wells Fargo & Company, Chick held senior leadership roles in several privately held firms.

Chick is a dynamic public speaker who engages the audience with insightful storytelling and a common sense approach to improving personal and organizational performance. Attendees describe Chick as possessing the unique ability to simplify complex situations and identify key activities that generate measurable results. Chick's approachable style allows him to quickly build high-trust relationships with leaders and create a safe environment for self-reflection, dialog and action.
Chick is an active community leader and is currently serving on the board of directors for Special Olympics Iowa. Chick lives in West Des Moines, IA with his wife and three sons.

Mike McCoy

Today, Mike McCoy advises, leads and invests in businesses that desire to achieve the next level of success. A dynamic financial services senior executive, his leadership experience spans early stage entrepreneurial organizations to Fortune 25 companies. Mike has a well-earned reputation for leading companies to superior performance combined with high employee engagement.

Before McCoy turned 30 years old he was leading a team of 2000 sales professionals. By age 40 he was head of distribution and chief marketing officer for a division of American Express. Before Mike turned 50 he was president of Wells Fargo consumer credit cards, a company with 4000+ team members, $20 billion in assets and a member of the Wells Fargo & Company Management Committee. During Mike's tenure he led the organization thru the depths of the recession with best in class performance coupled with outstanding employee engagement.

During his 10 year career with Wells Fargo & Company he led a number of businesses and functions including serving as EVP of Human Resources and Communications for a 50,000 person division of the company. McCoy's diverse background of leading teams, companies, and functions for both large and small companies has provided him with a unique strategic and operational perspective.

A frequent and sought after public speaker Mike connects with his audience through high energy and interactive presentations. Mike and his family live in Des Moines, IA where he is active in his community and church.